MINIATURE TO MASTERPIECE

Perfect Piecing Secrets from a Prizewinning Quiltmaker

Nancy Johnson-Srebro

RCW
PUBLISHING COMPANY

Miniature to Masterpiece©
Copyright © 1990 by Nancy Johnson-Srebro

Cover
"Never Again"
75" x 75"
Designed and pieced by Nancy Johnson-Srebro
Quilted by Debbie Grow
Photo courtesy of Chitra Publications

All other photography by Scott Mowry
Mowry Custom Photographic

Published by

Rebecca C. Wilber Publishing Company
RD#3, Old Post Lane
Columbia Crossroads, PA 16914-9535
(717)549-3333

ISBN 0-9627646-0-4

ACKNOWLEDGMENTS

Many thanks to Debbie Grow, who quilted all of my miniatures and quilts shown in this book and friend, Karen Brown, whose guidance is always appreciated.

I also wish to thank Peggy Schafer for her friendship and encouragement.

Without the help of students, Laurie Mace and Romayne Bonk, I couldn't have met the pattern deadline. Thank you.

A special thank you to Rebecca and Mark. Without their expertise, long hours and dedication to this project, Miniature to Masterpiece would not have been possible.

And my biggest thank you goes to my three children, Mark, Alan and Karen. Thank you for putting up with a quilting Mom!

DEDICATION

To my husband, Frank, and my friend, Jeanne.
Thank you for always being there.

TABLE OF CONTENTS

Introduction

"You make miniatures by machine?" It's a question I am often asked in disbelief. I laugh and try to explain the excitement of miniature making to them.

My enthusiasm goes way back. I can still remember when the highlight of coming home from school on Fridays was reading the *Grit Weekly*. For those of you who haven't heard of it, *Grit* featured a women's page of dress, crochet and quilt patterns. Quilt patterns held a special interest for me from about the earliest time I can remember. It's the same with quilting. The art has been a part of my life since early childhood. My strongest influence was my Grandma Garrison, who had twelve children, so she was always making quilts for bed coverings. With the time demands of a working farm, she tied her quilts with yarn. Grandma was thrilled when I expressed an interest in quilting. Over the years we would talk for hours about the newest designs that we found in the publications of that day. Today I realize what a lasting impact those talks have had on my life.

In my teenage years I put quilting on the back burner. Young adult interests occupied my life until I married my husband, Frank, in 1971. We transferred to California with the company he works for. For Christmas that year he bought me a White® sewing machine which I still use almost every day. I'd hate to try to estimate how many times its needle has gone up and down, or how many bobbins I've wound on it. The paint on its frame has been worn down to the metal, but it still purrs along with only an occasional oiling or adjustment. As I write this paragraph the White® is over eighteen years old. It has no fancy features. It's a basic machine and is well worn in, but it's all I need to make the smallest of miniatures! If you own a more modern machine, it may be used as well. However, a new machine isn't necessary - at least not with my techniques. You, too, can use the machine that you have.

Later, Frank and I moved to the East. We started a family and built a home. I worked part time for a few years. I didn't have much time left for quilt making, but I did make a few! For my first solo quilt I gathered all the material I owned, and borrowed some more from my mother. I cut out 6" squares using a template and scissors. Ignorance is bliss, I suppose. I used drapery fabric, poly blends, wool, double knits...there are only two or three pieces of 100% cotton in the whole quilt. But I love that quilt! It holds a lot of memories of my teenage years. The fabric patches trigger flashbacks of special times and places that mean a lot to me.

Looking back, 1984 is the year that marked the start of my career. My friend, Marty, gave me a cutting mat, rotary cutter and ruler for Christmas. I took my first and only quilting class. Our youngest child, Karen, started to attend school, which gave me more time to invest in quilt making. All of these factors conspired to get me started - but the new tools were probably the most important one. The new technology of the precision ruler and cutting equipment allowed me to cut pieces accurately. On reflection, I think the miniature quilt revolution is happening because of the development of these important tools. The finest accuracy of layout and cutting is within the reach of anyone who uses them. You can uniformly cut very small pieces. Size variation is reduced to a bare minimum. Piecing techniques have developed that take full advantage of this new equipment. Today, many folks are challenged by seeing how small they can go. And small they do go! I am a perfectionist when it comes to quilt piecing, and I know that the development of the rotary cutter, mat and ruler have made my career possible. Without these tools, quilting would still be a hobby for me, and *Miniature to Masterpiece* would not have been written.

After a few years the time came for new direction and growth. I had made over fifty quilts and was feeling the need for renewed challenge. I found it in miniature quilts. I started by reducing many of the traditional quilt patterns to the smallest size I thought was possible. Then I found ways to go even smaller. I pieced all of this work by machine. Next, I started developing original patterns. My miniatures were well received and I found that other quilters wanted to learn how to make them. This was the start of my teaching.

Teaching is especially gratifying to me, as I share the patterns and techniques I've developed myself. There aren't many teachers who offer guidance on miniature quilt making. This has been good for me as I have not been influenced by other teachers to any extent. For instance, since I have always done all of my piecing by machine, I didn't think twice about trying to sew 7/8 inch strips of fabric. And I found ways to do it effectively.

Having mastered miniatures, I challenged myself further to make a full size quilt from miniature blocks. I call this a "full size miniature quilt" - a term that's a bit contradictory - but there isn't any other phrase to describe it. The result was my "Wyoming"© quilt shown on page 36. To date, this quilt is recognized with two ribbons in national competition. I am now piecing my fifth full size-miniature quilt and find that it stimulates me to develop more and more intricate piecing patterns. This art form is a step or two beyond miniature quilt making. I've been fortunate to come along at the right time to help lead this evolution.

Why did I write this book? Basically it's to share my experience and techniques with you. In the following paragraphs I tell you *how* I present the information. Throughout *Miniature to Masterpiece*, I performed the delicate task of being exhaust*ive* without being exhaust*ing*. I fully expect that you will find all of the information that you need, with a sufficient, but not overpowering level of detail.

Miniature to Masterpiece treats the subject of miniature quilt piecing thoroughly, from start to finish. Virtually all of this guidance comes from my personal feelings and values. I have reflected on my thought processes when working through a new project, and present the chapters in the same sequence. The early chapters lay important groundwork on which the appeal and quality of your project depend. I have devoted many pages to fabric selection and the identification of practical color choices. The book progresses through a review of important information on the selection and techniques for use of your layout and cutting equipment. These have been written with miniature piecing in mind. Further chapters deal with setup and use of your sewing machine, to attain the ultimate in accuracy. I've also stressed some special pressing and pinning techniques that are necessary for miniature quilts. There are sections on quilting and binding of miniatures. The book concludes with a selection of twelve patterns that have been very popular with my students.

A special feature is a guide devoted to trouble-shooting your miniature piecing project. You may apply the principles to the patterns herein, or from another source. This practical guide is the result of countless hours of personal time spent working through problems that I've seen in my work. Hopefully, it will prevent you from hitting the same roadblocks that I have. The trouble-shooting section will definitely help with preventing *and* correcting problems with a minimum of time and effort on your part.

I devote the final section of *Miniature to Masterpiece* to what I call my full size, miniature quilts. Several folks have called them masterpieces, hence the name of this book. They are a step or two beyond either miniatures or conventional quilts. Of course, they include aspects of each. My miniature quilts contributed the intricacy of their piecing, and the finished size came from their conventional bed quilt ancestry. Techniques for making these masterpiece quilts are included in this book section.

To conclude my introduction, I'd like to offer all readers one bit of encouragement. Don't give up easily; think through your problems. I know the discouragement and frustration that comes from trying to put things together that just won't. The techniques and procedures described here work well for me and the thousands of students I have taught. Everything in *Miniature to Masterpiece* will work for you!

Practical Color Choices

One evening I walked past one of the Juniper shrubs that decorate the front of our home. I flushed a robin that startled me for an instant as she sped off. Thinking I would find her nest, I carefully parted the branches. Three blue-green eggs were nestled in the new, straw brown home they would occupy until the time was right to hatch. The dark brown of the inner branches set off the color of the nest. The green-blue of the Juniper needles finished the arrangement to perfection. What a superb sense of color our Creator must have!

The same thought flashed to me last fall as I looked out my studio window. It had been a glorious, golden day. The first pink rays of the sunset were bathing the ridge across from our home. The whole mountainside was a riot of color - the warm red of the oaks, the pastel yellow of the beeches and the muted scarlet of the maples. Here and there a patch of dark green hemlocks offset the combination with eye catching splendor. Suddenly, I felt very humble. The work of women and men is a poor substitute for the wonder of the world about us.

And how can we catch some of this color wonder in our quilts? All of us know that a good part of the appeal of our projects depends on the choice of colors. One of my basic rules is to always take the time to make the right selections. A miniature or full size quilt can't be undone very easily. Take your time choosing color, and don't make your choices lightly.

When I first started quilt making I read everything I could on the theory of color. Much of what I found had too much technical depth. The technical properties of color, such as hue, value and intensity, seem foreign and out of place in the fabric shop. This academic theory had marginal value to me when looking at hundreds of bolts of fabric in order to select three or four colors.

So what are we to do in choosing our colors? I've thought about my own color sense a great deal, so that I may logically explain it to students. I found that my own sense had evolved over time. Before I began teaching, I heard that some people are born with a so-called "good taste" for selecting appealing color combinations. This may be true but it's not to say that other folks who were not so blessed cannot develop the same ability. I've seen it happen in students over the course of a few projects. This can happen in different ways.

Inspiration is one of them. Look for and study objects that have good color appeal. What objects, you ask? Some that I have studied include the beautiful combinations that are often found in nature - scenery, flowers, shrubbery, even mineral deposits along the roadside. Inspiration can also occur in the art galleries. A study of the color combinations in many of the paintings on display, will highlight good matches to start with. One of my personal favorites is the morning sunrise and the evening sunset.

The colors of the atmosphere are never the same: appealing combinations are very common. You can also gain good insight from taking the time to study the beautiful colors in the shops and showroom windows. When clothes shopping I make it a point to keep my eyes open for exciting color matches on the mannequins. Advertising and display signs are also good sources. The colors in several of my quilts and some of my miniatures had this modest origin. To conclude, let me say that inspiration is one of those abstract words of which it is hard to catch the meaning. We may not even recognize that we've been inspired, even though it's happened.

Another way to help develop your color sense is to ask a "consultant" for her (or his) opinion. Over many years I have found that the folks who own or work in fabric shops are good contacts. Most all of them are very sincere and generous in sharing their perspectives on color matches. All you have to do is ask their opinion! Many of them handle a hundred times more fabric in one week than the average quilter will look at in a year. With this much hands-on experience your advisor has gained a conscious, or even subconscious, base to work from. Showing a copy of your pattern, and asking a two-step question, will get you a good perspective to start with. First, ask for the salesperson's opinion on a match or two for the theme color you want to go with. Show your pattern. After getting the recommendations, ask why she, or he, feels that this or that choice is good. You will get a variety of answers. It may be only their personal likes and dislikes. Other folks may share a step by step "process" that they've used to come up with the recommendation for your particular pattern. Usually, their logic makes sense. Consider the ones that do and condition yourself to think similarly. This sort of influence is a good teacher and the lessons you learn tend to stick well.

Most of the information in the preceding paragraphs deals with how to gain insight and influence your feelings on color. Now I'll move on and share my approach when I choose colors. Think of this as a step by step, practical approach. That's how I describe it to students. Obviously, my first step is to choose the pattern I will use. After making my selection, I then have to decide what its focal point **must be**, or **should be**. I say **must be** because there are some piecing patterns that force the eye to some key piece in each block. It may even be the background. What is it? That's what I have to determine. Generally, it doesn't make sense to try to highlight another piece with my lightest or darkest color. At other times, the pattern doesn't tell me what it's focal point must be, and I have to decide what it **should be**. What should the eyes focus on when looking at the miniature or quilt block? Study the pattern carefully. Should the background tie everything together, or is there some other piece that would do it better? Here's where some intuition comes into play. Mentally, pick some bold color and visualize it in different pieces of each block. Do the same exercise with your color in the background, and lattice strips if you will use them. It might be helpful to photocopy the pattern and use colored pencils or crayons to try to locate the focal piece. Please remember, right now you're not trying to choose colors. The only decision you need to make is what piece of the pattern will be your focal point. Usually, the answer comes easily. Again, this decision will identify the piece that demands the viewer's attention. Here is where I will use my lightest or darkest color shade.

Next, I must decide whether to go lightest or darkest shade for this piece. This is largely a matter of personality, and your

likes and dislikes. Your mood may even enter the picture. At times I find that I am a light shade person, and other times I tend to go with the darker shades. Move right through this decision. If it feels right, go for it! In miniature quilt making you get a quick turn-around on the project. You can easily make two miniatures that complement each other. For one, use a light shade for the focal piece. Go with a dark shade for the other. Compare the two miniatures. The result will astound you.

Most times, I use my lightest and darkest shades in pieces that adjoin each other. This increases the effect of the color shades, and helps keep the focus where you want it to be in the completed block - especially true in miniature making.

This brings me to actual selection of the colors. My first choices are the lightest and darkest shades. Usually, I have something in mind for one or the other. It might be the color of the room where I will display the miniature. Perhaps it's the recipient's favorite color if I'm piecing a gift. At times I've stayed with a certain color when making a series of miniatures, or it might even be a color that I haven't used in a while, something to change the pace. All of these have caused me to start with a certain color for the focus. Next, I choose its counterpart. If I know the light shade, I get on with finding the dark, and vice versa. I try to remember that light and dark are relative to each other. For instance, a medium blue would be dark relative to a pink, but light relative to a red. For a dazzling, eyecatching look I will go with a wide range from light to dark. For instance, in the preceding example I might use pink as the light and red as the dark. However, if I am looking for a more subtle, conservative effect I would narrow the range. It might be pink for the light and medium blue for the dark.

How do you decide to go with either the dazzling or the conservative look, or maybe even the midrange? That's easy. You may not even have to think about it. When teaching I have seen a good correlation between the shades of colors worn by my students, and the fabrics they are using. Usually, if a student is wearing bright colors with a lot of shade contrast, her project fabrics follow suit. The opposite also occurs, with conservative color ranges in her wardrobe and in the fabrics for the class. I've seen this correlation in class enough times to be able to predict the student's project colors with good accuracy. My own closet is full of clothes that are in shades of red, blue, beige and black. I find these colors easiest for me to work with because I have been living with them so long. When making miniatures on speculation, I frequently shift from wide range of shades, to narrow range. Why? It boils down to having an idea of the effect I'm trying to create. If I want something to catch the eye and demand attention as soon as someone comes into the room, it's a wide range. Increasingly milder "attention getters" require less and less range of color shades.

Let me recap where I'm at right now in this process. I started my project knowing what my theme color or colors (two) will be. In reviewing my pattern I have decided on its focal point piece. Next, I decided whether the focal piece will be lightest or darkest. See Bear's Paw miniature, page 41. Whichever it is, the adjoining piece will usually be the opposite. Keeping the desired effect in mind (bold or conservative), I then select another color to set the other end of the shade range. This may be my second theme color if I already have one in mind. Throughout this section, please keep in mind that the word "shade" is used. This refers to the contrast between light and dark. I sometimes use an example to describe shade to students. Make a photocopy of a colored photograph of a quilt. You will get a black, white and gray copy of the colors in the photograph. The contrast between the white, grays and blacks is plain to see. This is shade.

Next, I move on to selecting my medium color. Referring to shade, it will be about halfway between my light and dark colors. This is where inspiration and color sense you have developed come into play. There is one watchout!! The shade range between the lightest and darkest colors must not be too narrow. Using three colors within a narrow shade range will usually guarantee a flat, non-inspiring miniature or quilt. I take a look at the three colors I have tentatively selected - light, medium and dark. I view them from across the room so I can have a better perspective. Is there a fair difference in shades? What would these three fabrics look like if I photocopied swatches of them all together? If I think they will look too flat I deliberately put the light or dark away, choosing an even lighter or darker color. Then I go back to choosing my medium color.

My final step is the one I call "the fun step." Now I know what my three basic colors will be. Assuming that my project requires five or six colors, I can now start looking at different hues of these three basic colors. For instance - beige compared with a brown, or medium blues compared with a navy. The differences may not be as broad as in these examples. It depends, of course, on the three basic colors that I have selected. This is the step where you will gain what I call the personality of the miniature or quilt. I find that it is comparatively easy to choose my basic colors. The selection of the contrasting hues takes more time, but is definitely more fun!

Color Choice Model

I have found that a model is helpful in portraying the logic that I use to make my color choices. It's easy to follow. Start at the top and move downward through the various steps with their prompting questions. This is my model for practical color choices for miniatures and quilts.

Model for Practical Color Choices

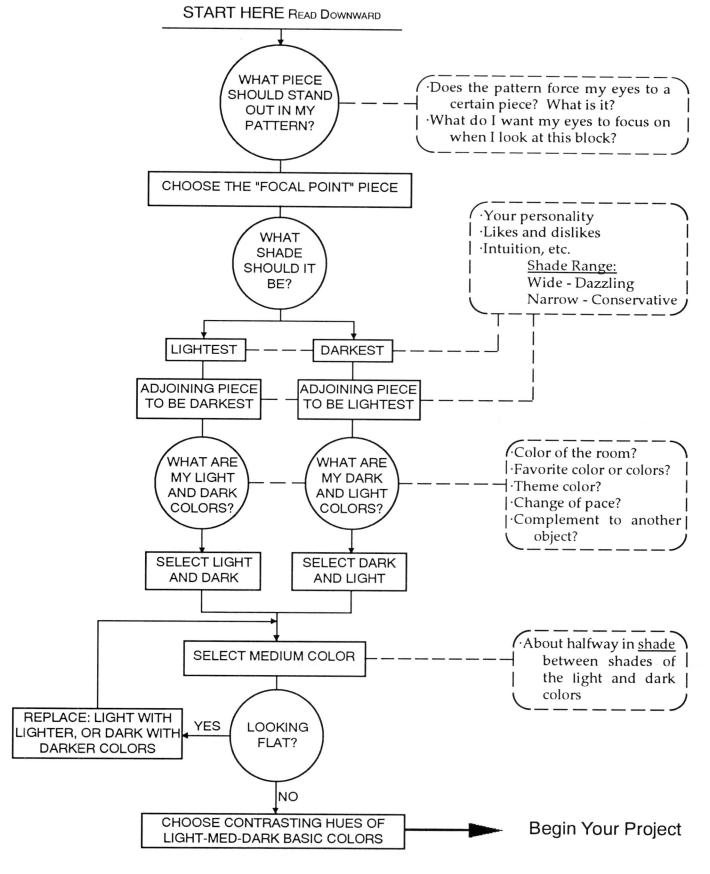

START HERE Read Downward

WHAT PIECE SHOULD STAND OUT IN MY PATTERN?

· Does the pattern force my eyes to a certain piece? What is it?
· What do I want my eyes to focus on when I look at this block?

CHOOSE THE "FOCAL POINT" PIECE

WHAT SHADE SHOULD IT BE?

· Your personality
· Likes and dislikes
· Intuition, etc.
  Shade Range:
  Wide - Dazzling
  Narrow - Conservative

LIGHTEST — DARKEST

ADJOINING PIECE TO BE DARKEST

ADJOINING PIECE TO BE LIGHTEST

WHAT ARE MY LIGHT AND DARK COLORS?

WHAT ARE MY DARK AND LIGHT COLORS?

· Color of the room?
· Favorite color or colors?
· Theme color?
· Change of pace?
· Complement to another object?

SELECT LIGHT AND DARK

SELECT DARK AND LIGHT

SELECT MEDIUM COLOR

· About halfway in shade between shades of the light and dark colors

REPLACE: LIGHT WITH LIGHTER, OR DARK WITH DARKER COLORS

YES

LOOKING FLAT?

NO

CHOOSE CONTRASTING HUES OF LIGHT-MED-DARK BASIC COLORS

Begin Your Project

Fabric Selection

I have three simple rules that I apply when selecting fabrics for miniature making:

1. Use 100% cotton
2. Use 100% cotton
3. Use 100% cotton

I realize that always using cotton fabrics may be controversial, but that's how I think. I am a traditionalist at heart. You can see it clearly in my home decor, its furnishings and in my quilts and miniatures. I recognize the utility value of using man made fibers in clothing, drapery, and carpeting. However, I avoid using them in miniatures and quilts. Cotton was the fiber that women used when quilt making started. To me, it's the tie that brings my creations back home to their roots.

I'm sure that some of you who are reading this book lean toward the contemporary. If you do, great! All of us are individuals, we don't ever want to stifle our creativity by blindly following someone's lead all the time. Over the years I have seen many outstanding quilts that were made of polyester and other manufactured fibers. Can you use them in miniatures? Definitely yes - it's up to you.

Assuming that you want to use cotton, make sure that the bolt's label says 100% and that the weaving pattern is tight. Tight means that many individual threads are woven together. There are different grades of 100% cotton. Some are woven more tightly than others. The loose ones do not work well for miniatures. You can gain a good understanding of this through a comparison. Choose four to six swatches of cotton fabric from different manufacturers. Depending on your samples, you should see a difference in the tightness of the weave. The looser ones tend to fray easily when handling the cut pieces. They may distort and start to unravel when ironing. Make a conscious effort to go with the ones that are more tightly woven.

Large or Small Scale Fabric

Throughout the chapter on practical color choices I have deliberately avoided any reference to fabric scale. By scale I am referring to the percentage of an offsetting color, because of the presence of a print on the fabric. A solid color, obviously, has no scale - it's just 100% red, blue, green or whatever. On the other hand, any fabric has some scale if it has two or more colors and a visible pattern. For instance, a fabric with a fine vine, tiny floral design or small pin dots would be small scale in my terminology. Conversely, if the fabric has large flowers, wide stripes, or big dots, it would be large scale. There's also a "middle of the road" scale that's between the two ranges. Let's deal only with the two extremes - large scale or small scale, for now.

LARGE SCALE

I think it is wise to avoid using large scale fabrics in the body of the quilt block. This guidance is based on my experience with miniatures, and my latest work on full-size, miniature quilts. Typically, I use large scale prints only in my borders and sometimes in my background. There are exceptions to every rule of course, but this is one I rarely deviate from. Why? There are some good reasons. Using large scale prints within the block conflicts with the concept of miniatures. Often times, the person looking at a large scale fabric intermixed with small scales has the impression that the quilter made a mistake. Perhaps she couldn't find anything better suited. I've also seen where a large scale print in the body of the block will trigger a distraction from the overall effect of the pattern. Large scale prints also demand more time in the cutting and sewing stages, to maintain a symmetrical look. I rarely use large scale prints in the body of the block. When I do, it is to create a deliberate eye catcher that I want to have for some reason.

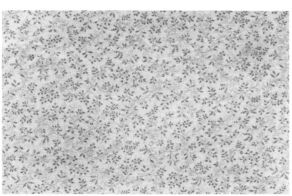

SMALL SCALE

On the other hand, if you use all small scale prints the miniature will lean toward being dull and boring. This will happen despite your best efforts at color selection for the effect you are trying to create.

By now the reader has probably concluded that I make some use of medium scale prints. I have found that a good way to avoid the problems described here is to use one or two medium scale prints to complement your small prints. However, I rarely use more than two. Although the eye may not register it, the overall effect is that the miniature is difficult to make. It looks more complex than it really is. The medium print makes the small scale prints look even smaller. This conveys a very desirable effect to anyone looking at the miniature quilt.

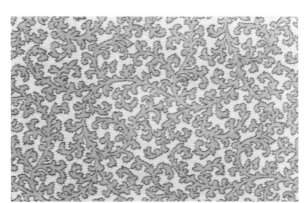

MEDIUM SCALE

There is another topic that relates to fabric scale. Should you use fabrics that have more than one off-setting color in their printed design? For instance, as I write this I am looking at a quilter's quarter that has an off white background, and a delicate tree branch and leaf pattern. The print is light blue, and it has occasional clumps of cranberry colored berries, that are no larger than the head of a pin. As I've described it I'm sure it sounds very busy. In reality the small scale of the print design makes the fabric look light gray from beyond a few feet. Will I use it in a miniature? Definitely! I have no aversion to using multicolored prints in the body of my blocks. In fact, I am constantly searching for small scale fabric that has more than one off-setting color. The motive is simple. The miniature will look more complex and therefore more desirable.

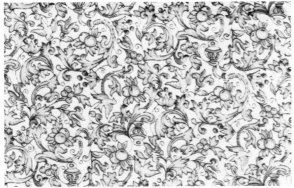

OFF-SETTING PRINTS

I'd like to finish this section on fabric scale with one final thought. I've found that in miniature piecing, as in many other aspects of life, there are few rigid rules. The best that I, or any author or teacher, can do is to offer guidelines. They will give you a good start. From that point on, your individual taste should take over. If it looks good, go for it! Often times I have tried something different, usually on purpose, and have been pleasantly surprised. Don't limit yourself.

Fabric Preparation

I remember a class a few years ago when one of my students was making a feathered star wallhanging. Her colors were outstanding, she was doing a superb job with the piecing and I was happy for her. The next time I saw her, I asked how the quilting was going. Her reaction told me something was wrong. She replied how disappointed she was. In the process of quilting it she got a stain on her block (remember to keep those chocolate candy bars away from your project). After finishing the quilting, she washed it. Imagine her surprise when she saw that one of the colors had run into the light background! We talked about the prewashing instructions that we had reviewed in class. In the excitement of starting the wallhanging she hadn't taken the time to do it. What a painful lesson to learn.

A good rule is to prewash every piece of fabric that you will be using in your project. I use a powdered detergent, Tide®, and it works well. I make sure that the granules dissolve before putting my fabric in the washer. Why? To make sure that none of the fabric sees a high concentration of detergent even for a short period of time. From the washer, all the fabric goes into the dryer. By doing this I make sure that it is preshrunk. This is to avoid problems that might come up later if you must wash your miniature or quilt.

Next I get into pressing. I use a dry iron and a spray product called Magic® Sizing, which I buy in the larger grocery stores. This step will smooth out the wrinkles and restore body. This is important throughout the layout and cutting of the individual pieces of your block.

I'd like to leave this section with a suggestion from a personal experience. Don't let your unwashed fabric collect. If you're a "fabric-oholic" you'll eventually forget what's been prewashed and what hasn't. So you'll end up prewashing and ironing everything again, to make sure. Also, it's easier and less time consuming to wash and iron in small batches. One semester I was teaching a heavy schedule. I bought a lot of fabric on speculation, and didn't prewash any of it because of time demands. At the end of the semester I had eight washer loads. And the hardest part was there were eight clothes baskets of fabric to iron!

Equipment

Much of the quality and appeal of your miniature or quilt rests on your choice of equipment, and your techniques in using it. Both of these become more critical as you get into smaller and smaller miniatures.

A comparison I often use is one that I'm sure many of us can relate to. As I'm sure you know, home paneling that you install on your walls usually comes in sheets that measure 48" wide and 96" long. This is roughly one half of the width of a full size quilt. An experienced carpenter can do a superb job in paneling a room using nothing more than a common tape measure and hand saw. This equipment gives all the accuracy that's needed. On the other hand, the same tape measure and saw would hardly do to build a frame for a memorable photograph. Even with the same craftsman using them. And so it is with miniature making; you must have accurate measuring and cutting equipment if you will do splendid work. The more accurate your equipment, the better your work. It's that simple!

Ruler

I have no reservations in recommending one of the product lines that are out on the market - Omnigrid's® rulers. When I first saw one of their rulers I remember thinking "who needs all of these markings?" I felt that all I needed for miniature quilt making was a transparent straight edge with some fractional inch markings. And I already owned a ruler that worked okay. But, I'm not one for dismissing new ideas easily. I did take the time to study the Omnigrid® ruler. It appeared to have some special features that would give me an edge. I bought one to test, being pleased with what I found out. Its horizontal and vertical markings let me "square up" my pieced block if needed. One feature that is outstanding is the black markings with the yellow highlighting. I find that I am more apt to position the edge of my fabric exactly under the black line. Like a traffic signal, maybe the yellow makes me more cautious or careful.

Another aspect of the Omnigrid® product is a life saver to me, and it may be the same for other quilters. About two years ago I had to undergo wrist surgery for Carpal Tunnel Syndrome. The yellow lines on the underside of the ruler helps immensely. It increases the friction between the fabric and the ruler. The ruler "stays put" without heavy hand pressure. This allows me to concentrate on my layout and cutting, maintaining high accuracy despite my wrists.

One final word on the product. Accuracy! Since trying my first Omnigrid® ruler I've bought more of them in all different sizes and shapes. Often times, I use more than one Omnigrid® ruler during a project. I have no problems when I interchange the rulers.

Some words of caution: whatever name ruler you use, stay with it throughout your sewing project. You don't want to chance having piecing problems because of a variation in ruler markings.

Rotary Cutter

Over the years I've tried several different brands of rotary cutters. I keep coming back to the yellow Olfa® cutter. It is made very well and it holds up well under heavy use. Also, because of its design you can easily see where the blade is during the cutting process. I don't like to waste material and this lets me be efficient. I don't have to cut well beyond my edge line, just to make sure.

On a safety note, remember that the blade wheel is very sharp. Always keep its guard in place, at all times except when actually cutting. Remember to flick the guard back over the blade wheel as soon as you finish a cut. Soon this will become a habit. Treat your rotary cutter with respect.

Be careful not to drop your rotary cutter. Also, watch for pins while you are cutting. Because its wheel is so sharp, it will nick easily. This will break a tiny chip out of the metal. Whenever that chip contacts the fabric it will not cut a thread or two. Then when you try to lift or separate your fabric, you can't. The uncut thread holds everything together, causing your fabric to shift. This makes for very inaccurate cutting.

I like to replace my cutter blades frequently. With use, the blade becomes dull. You may not even notice the difference while it's happening. Eventually the wheel gets so dull that it's causing obvious cutting problems. I keep this from happening by marking the date on the wheel when I install it. This is a constant reminder that triggers a replacement when I think it's time. How much time between changes? It depends on my schedule and how much I've used my rotary cutter. Another advantage of frequent blade changes is that it lowers the stress on my hands. I can use less pressure to get a clean cut. Also - keep those old blades for cutting your plastic or cardboard piecing templates. They're also good for cutting wallpaper and when your son or daughter comes home with a sheet of school pictures.

Cutting Board

For three years I used a green mat that had little dimples all over it. I wore the center out and it started to shed little green flakes on everything. I bought a smooth mat and could not believe how much longer my rotary cutter blade stayed sharp. I used this cutting board for two years until Omnigrid® came out with a reversible cutting mat. It is green on one side, for working with light fabrics. The opposite side is white for use with dark fabrics. This is a great idea! The shade contrast helps me because I tend to concentrate more closely on the fabric during the cutting phase. This, in turn, reduces the size variation in the pieces I have cut. Why should all the pieces have a uniform size? I recall a sign that I once saw in an antique furniture shop. Its legend said: "Condition is everything". Applied to miniature quilt making, my version would be: "Accuracy is everything".

I want to finish this section with a comment on cutting boards. Although I've tried them, I have not found a use for gridded mats. To me, it's confusing and unnecessary to work with two scales or grids. Why would you need one on your ruler and another one on your mat? I have always been able to achieve high cutting accuracy with my ruler alone. Often a student who owns a gridded mat will ask me if she should use it for miniature quilt making. Definitely! Just ignore the size markings on the mat or use the reverse side of the mat. Depend on your ruler during the cutting.

How To Use Your Equipment

This section will describe my techniques in using the ruler, rotary cutter and cutting board. I am right handed. Left handed readers should keep this in mind, doing the opposite when I mention a specific hand placement.

Over the years I've refined my own techniques, mostly through trial and error. To teach what I do, I have put together the following cutting exercise.

Cutting Exercise

Your cutting board should be on a firm, sturdy table that has extra room for material, your rotary cutter and instructions and so forth. Select a piece of fabric. Pretend that it is from a full width bolt, which is 44". This dimension will be helpful when you refer to the diagrams. Fold your fabric in half so both of the selvages are on one side. Place it on your cutting board with the fold at the top (farthest away from you). The selvages will be at the bottom, nearest to you. See Figure 1.

Now, place your ruler's short side (6") along the fold line. Do this as accurately as you can. The long side (24") will be parallel with the right hand edge. It will be opposite if you are left handed. Take care to position your ruler edge so that you will only trim a small amount from the edge when you cut. There is no sense in wasting fabric. I usually trim 1/4 inch or less. See Figure 2.

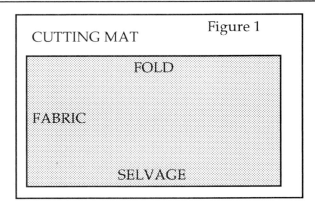

Place your left hand on the bottom six inches of the ruler. Start cutting at the bottom with the blade against the ruler. Cut until the cutter wheel is even with the tips of your fingers. Stop cutting. Now, move your hand up the ruler another six inches. Continue cutting until the cutter is again even with your fingertips. Stop again and continue as before, in steps, until you cut through the fold.

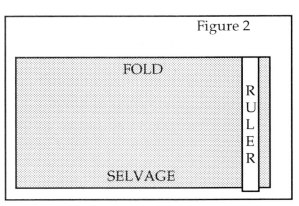

I have found that my hand-walking method works very well. If you try to make a long cut in one pass, there is a good chance that the ruler will move. The cutter presses against the side of the ruler and causes it to pivot away from the pressure. As a result, the cut is not straight. If you try to use less side pressure against the ruler, the cutter tends to wander away in the opposite direction. The result is the same. The edge is not straight. By stopping two or three times and moving your hand up the ruler, you are almost guaranteed to get a perfect cut.

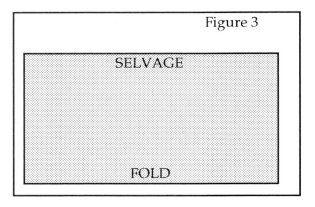

After you have cut your straight edge, turn the board 180 degrees, one half of a full turn. Do not try to turn the fabric on the board. It is too easy to disturb the newly cut edge. This straight edge will now be on your left. The fold will be at the bottom of the board, nearest to you. See Figure 3.

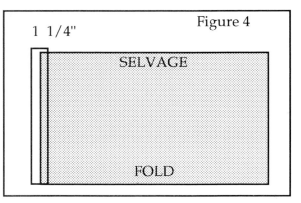

Now, you can begin to cut the strips. Let's say you want a strip 1 1/4" wide by 44" long. Position the long side of your ruler exactly over the straight edge that you had cut before. Since the ruler's markings are parallel, you are now ready to cut a uniform 1 1/4" strip. Remember to move your hand up the ruler several times during the cut. See Figure 4.

Omnigrid's® rulers are especially good when you are cutting strips. Every 1/4" you will see a solid line. Other rulers only have solid lines on the full inch markings. Since you will often cut pattern pieces to fractional sizes, this can be a real advantage.

After cutting three or four strips, I will **always** resquare the large piece of fabric. To do this, just turn your cutting board 180 degrees and repeat the procedure that you started with. I cannot overemphasize the importance of this step. If you are cutting many strips and you do not resquare, your strips will develop a "V" at the fold line. You will have problems later with any piece that you cut from the centerpart of your strips.

I avoid using templates whenever possible. As you will see, most of my patterns do not require their use. The reason is simple. I have found through experience that templates can be a source of inaccuracy. Remember my "Accuracy is everything" comment a few pages back?

The smaller your miniature quilt, the more accurate your pieces must be. Here is how inaccuracy comes into the picture. If you are using a template, you must remember that its designer used a certain size pencil or pen for marking. You may, and probably will, be using something different for marking. Depending on what you use, your cutting line will be closer to (or farther away from) the template's outline. Even though it is a very small difference, the differences will collect when you sew many small pieces together. For example, a one one-hundred inch oversize on each piece will add up to 1/2 inch when you sew 50 pieces together. The opposite may happen if you use a marker that has a finer point than the pattern designer used. In the example cited here, the finished size of the block would be one half inch smaller. If you are using a pencil for marking, the piece will become larger as the pencil point becomes duller. You must remember to keep it sharpened for uniform marking.

Because of this problem, I have designed my patterns to use templates only as a last resort. I will use my ruler to cut squares, rectangles and triangles whenever possible. I can even cut hexagons for a Grandma's Flower Garden, and octagons for the patterns that use them.

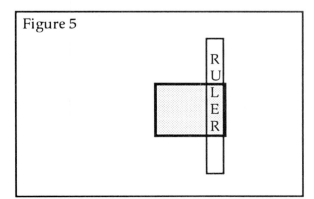

Figure 5

Finally, there are just times when you must use a marking instrument. If I do have to draw around a template, I use an extra fine point Sharpie® black marking pen. The black color is a good highlighter for most fabrics, and the marking pen's point doesn't become dull during use. Be sure to select one that has an extra fine point. It should have a cone shaped point that is hard plastic or metal, not felt or similar material. The finer the drawn line, the better. Then use your ruler and rotary cutter, not scissors, to cut **inside** the drawn shape. Be sure to cut off the fine black line. If you don't, you have increased the size of your piece. See Figure 5.

Your Sewing Machine

In the Introduction, I explained that I do all my piecing with an older White® sewing machine. My students and friends use everything from vintage Singers™ to the ultra modern machines that are now on the market. Good results may be had with all of them. Miniature quilt making requires only the basic sewing stitch, which all machines can do well.

There are some special things to keep in mind when you use your machine. Here are a few of them:

Needle

I find that a size 11 needle is essential for precision piecing of miniatures. This is very important and I always stress it to students. A size 14 or larger needle tends to mangle your small pieces. The diameter difference is small, but the effect is huge. You want to pierce the fabric as cleanly as possible, not just push through. The size 11 needle will do it. Also, I replace my needle after 15 hours of sewing. Its point will become dull and you can see the difference after you put a new needle in the machine.

Presser Foot

When I started making miniatures, I experimented with several types of presser feet. I found that the so-called "applique foot" works well.The large open area allows you to see exactly what's going on while you sew your fabric. You can monitor stitch length and tension continuously. This is more important in miniature quilt making, than in any other sewing that I am familiar with.

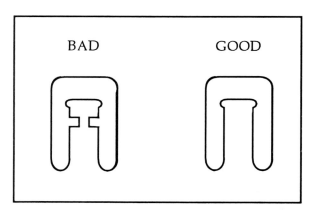

Before I found the applique foot, I experimented with several feet to increase their open area. A plea to my husband, Frank, had him fooling with a small metal file. Presto! A presser foot especially made for the needs of miniature makers. If you can't find an applique foot for your machine, you may want to try the same modification. Be careful not to leave any burrs or rough edges that will catch on your fabric as you sew.

Sewing Guide

Let me start this section by commenting on seam width. I routinely use a 1/4" seam allowance even for the smallest of miniatures. Occasionally, I'll use a 3/16" seam allowance. It's not that I haven't experimented with 1/8" allowances. I found that I had to help feed my fabric with a large quilting pin or similar object. This was time consuming and control was difficult during sewing. My seam allowance accuracy suffered. Because of this I reverted to using mostly 1/4" seams for my miniature and quilt piecing.

I have had students tell me that the outside of their machine's presser foot is exactly 1/4" from the needle point. Sometimes it is. At other times it is not; close but not exactly 1/4" (as it must be). Because of this, I always set up my student's machines with sewing guides for accurate control of seam width. Do not rely on your presser foot.

When I started miniature teaching I saw students using a surprising variety of sewing guide set-up techniques. Most of them worked, but involved a lot of trial and error. I developed a quick but effective method that uses 1/4" masking tape. I thought my idea was ingenious until I saw a variation of my method a few years later in a quilting book! After setting up literally thousands of sewing machines this way, I can vouch for the masking tape method without reservation.

Put your needle down until it is just starting to enter the hole in the throat plate. Cut a piece of 1/4" wide masking tape that is about 6" long. Next, lay the tape against the tip of the needle, perpendicular to the long axis of your machine. Stick it in place.

At this point the student starts to get excited and says, "But my dog feet won't work!" I ask them to be patient and trust me.

Next I stick another piece of 1/4" masking tape against the length of the first piece. Then pull off the first piece of tape. The second piece is spaced exactly 1/4" from the tip of the needle. You will always have a perfect 1/4" seam allowance if you take care to feed your fabric with its edge against the tape. Correct? Not always!

During my first year of teaching I had a group of 16 students in class. I showed each of them how well this method works, and they all thought I was great. Then Murphy's Law entered the picture and burst my bubble! After sewing for two hours, it was obvious that some of the students' projects were not turning out right. At first I could not determine the cause. I had set up everyones' sewing guides and I knew that their cutting was accurate. A bit of detective work uncovered the problem. I found out that the 1/4" masking tape was not a true 1/4"! I had run out of tape on one roll and used another roll to finish the set ups. The second roll was close to 1/4" wide, but not right on. I learned a lesson the hard way. Before beginning your miniature, always sew a double thickness of scrap fabric. Take care to butt it against the sewing guide tape. To check your seam allowance after sewing, place your ruler on top of the fabric. Take care to place the edge of your ruler even with the straight edge of your fabric. Its 1/4" marking should be exactly on top of your stitches. If the ruler marking does not coincide with your stitches, just move your sewing guide tape to the right or left. Only a slight adjustment is necessary. Again try a double thickness of fabric to check the 1/4" seam allowance. Repeat this procedure until you verify that you have a 1/4" seam allowance.

Once you are sure of this, build up the sewing guide with several layers of 3/4" masking tape. The reason for using 3/4" wide tape is because it is much sturdier and longer lasting than 1/4" tape. On my own sewing machine I have gone to using packaging or filament tape. It is thicker and lasts longer under heavy use. By putting several layers of tape on your original strip, you will be able to butt your fabric next to it. If you use only one layer of tape, your fabric tends to ride slightly over the strip of tape.

It is also good practice to verify your seam allowance periodically, even if you haven't changed anything. This will check for a bent needle or other unforseen problems.

Sewing

Sewing techniques for miniature quilts are simple and straight forward. All you need to know is how to operate your sewing machine. I'm sure that many, if not most of you, have already mastered this. Building on this assumption, there are only two factors that I will elaborate on here.

The first one is attention. You must pay careful attention to what's going on between the presser foot and throat plate on your machine. Once again, accuracy is essential. Check your tension and seam allowance frequently. Don't rush through your project. The few extra minutes invested in extra attention during sewing will pay off in the quality of your finished quilt top.

Secondly, a few hints are in order:

Stitch length - in miniature or quilt work I always use 10 to 12 stitches per inch. You will sometimes be sewing long strips together and then recutting them into very small pieces. If you have too few stitches, the small pieces will start to come apart during handling. As I teach more students I am finding that this is a common problem experienced by miniature makers.

Chain Piecing

Some of you may not be familiar with chain piecing. With this technique you can sew sets of squares, etc., one after another without removing them from your machine. After a series of pieces you will end up with a "chain" that has the individual units just barely joined together.

Try to chain piece whenever possible. It will save you loads of time and your seams will be straighter and more accurate. Why? I 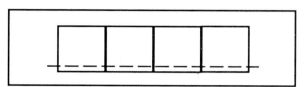 think it's because you are subconsciously looking at the stitch line on the preceding pieces, as you sew the new one. Your tendency is to sew the new piece just like the one or two before it.

A common comment I hear from students is that their machine will not chain piece triangles. I have always used the following method for chain piecing triangles. It works well on all the machines that I have tried it with.

Be sure to butt the fabric against your sewing guide, and sew almost to the end of the triangle. Try to stop about 1/8 inch from the point. If the needle is not down, cycle the machine by hand until the needle is down through the fabric. Lift the presser foot up and insert your next piece, overlapping slightly. Don't get excited because the tips of your triangles overlap. You will be cutting the tips off later. Then put your presser foot down and start sewing. This method works great for those machines that balk at chain piecing triangles. I find that it works every time!

To chain piece squares, rectangles and similar polygons you can use the same procedure, with one exception. Usually, you won't have 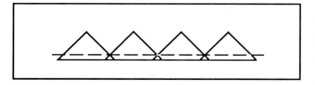 to lift the presser foot between the pieces. Just sew almost to the end of the piece and butt the next square right up to the sewn square. By chain piecing this way your needle is always sewing on your fabric, never in thin air.

Pressing

If there is only one secret section written into the pages of Miniature to Masterpiece, many of you have just found it! Pressing is a critical part of miniature and quilt making. I cringe when I see quiltmakers, with years of experience, using an iron like a rolling pin on heavy dough!

I have found that many of my students are capable of making a good miniature quilt, before taking a class. The class provides the pattern and "walk through" instructions. When I counsel students on pressing, the light bulbs come on! I hear tales and legends of past projects that just didn't work out. Typically, it was a pucker or a seam that would not line up. Usually these folks find out that they've been too aggressive in pressing their piecing. I tell my students not to press down heavily on the iron; let your hand guide the iron and press lightly. My pressure analogy is to compare the push broom for your garage, and the feather duster for your china cabinet.

Also, I never press with steam. Right now I can hear the hue and cry of all you steam lovers. Steam doesn't work for me. I have found through experience that steam really stretches some 100% cottons. I'm not sure why this is, but I know that it happens. I have my iron set on the dry/cotton setting and this works out fine. On the other hand, if you use steam and it works, go for it. As they say, the proof is in the pudding.

Another technique that I always use is to press on the right side of the fabric. By right side, I mean the side that you will see when you look at your miniature quilt. By doing this you will see what your finished piece will look like, as you go.

Students who learned to press on the wrong (back) side, usually like this technique after they have tried it. It does have advantages over the wrong side pressing method.

Readers of *Miniature to Masterpiece* undoubtedly have a good understanding of my quilt piecing philosophy by now. Don't limit your thinking. I tell students to try every different way of cutting, sewing and pressing they can find or dream up themselves. Find the ways that work for you, and keep trying to improve them through experimenting.

A hint that fits in the pressing section is to never, but never, cut your pieces from wrinkled fabric. I know that we all are anxious to get into that pile of fabric and start cutting. If you don't press before cutting your pieces, they will grow in size when pressed. Now you have pieces that are larger than the pattern calls for.

Pressing Squares Made From Two Triangles

When I first started making miniatures, I ran into problems pressing a square made from two triangles. I thought that if you sewed the two triangles together along the diagonal, and pressed to the dark, everything would be fine. Logically, as a final step you would cut off those pesky tips, which many folks call "dog ears".

However, in reality when I tried this I found that the miniature squares would not stay square. They tend to elongate and become very slightly diamond-shaped. This is enough to matter when making miniature quilts. After thinking this one through, I figured it out.

Both triangles are symmetrical during the sewing. However, when pressing to the dark, the square is unsymmetrical. The heat and pressure deform the two halves differently. After experimenting, I developed the following method which I have since shared with thousands of students:

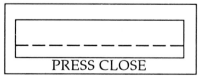

Sew your triangle together along the diagonal side.

Next you should cut off the tips (dog ears) **before** proceeding.

Now, open up the square with the right side facing you. Have your seam allowance towards the dark fabric. Using your two thumbs press down on the diagonal seam while checking to make sure your square is square. Put your square on the ironing board and position your iron on top of the square. You will let the heat of the iron do the work for you. No movement of the iron is necessary, or even desirable. I also use this method for making regular squares for full size quilts.

On occasion, students ask me about a grid system for making a square from two triangles. I have tried this method and found that it doesn't work as well for me. However, if this system works for you, use it. The bottom line is that your squares must be truly square. You can find the grid method in alternate books and magazines.

Setting Your Seams

This topic is important enough to review in detail. About five years ago I was having a terrible time making a Double Irish Chain Quilt. I couldn't get my short strips pressed just right. They had a slight bow after pressing instead of being nice and straight. My tension was correct on the machine, so I wasn't sure what was going on. I tried pressing several different ways. Finally, I developed the following method. Press your seam closed, as it comes off the machine. Then open the two fabrics right side facing you and press again toward the dark. Presto! It worked like magic.

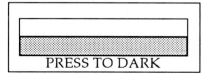

This technique eases any stresses caused by the machine tension. You will get this stress even if your tension is correct. By setting your seams you will reduce the tendency toward puffiness in your strips. I also use this method when joining blocks, lattice strips and borders. Any time my piece is longer than 2", I set the seam. I teach this technique in class and it is an instant success.

Pressing Long Strips

Occasionally, you will want to piece long strips. When pressing, the strip will try to form a curve even if you set the seam. To lessen this tendency, I use this technique. First, set the seam. Next, separate the two layers of fabric so you are looking at the right side. Start in the center of your strip. Use your fingers to gently press about four inches of fabric to the dark side. Finally, take your iron and gently press with a back and forth motion. Do not press crosswise or diagonally. Continue with this procedure, in approximate 4" increments, until you come to the end of the strip.

Press the other half of your strip in the same way. Be sure to start at the center and work toward the end in steps. This method will assure you of getting a nice, straight strip. I have used this method literally thousands of times and I still smile when I see the results.

PRESS IN THIS DIRECTION

Pinning

All pins are the same, right? Not by me! Through trial and error I have found what I believe to be the perfect pin for making miniatures and quilts. This is the #104 fine silk pin, by the W.H. Collins Company. I love this long, thin pin. I discovered it while working through one of the first difficulties I faced with miniatures. Pinning was a problem. All of the pins I tried would leave a hump where I pinned several layers together. After sewing a seam, and removing the pins, I could always see where the pin had been. The stitching in the hump area would be different than in the rest of the seam. Usually, you see a small pucker due to the machine tension. Another problem is a slight bend to the right or left (directionally) in the stitching. Occasionally, the machine needle would hit the pin squarely, bending or breaking it. I'm sure many of you can relate to this problem, as I've heard it hundreds of times from students. Since the hump was causing the problem, I reasoned that I'd have to eliminate it or make it smaller. Pinning is a necessity; there is no way around it. So I started looking for a pin that had a very small diameter. After a lot of searching, I found the Collin's Fine Silk Pins. I tried a box and found that it leaves no hump. I can sew over it without difficulty, it's long and thin and oh so sharp. I had found my pin!

Seam Layout

Whether you are working from a pattern, or designing your own miniature quilt, you have to consider how the seams will lay in your finished block. Looking at the wrong side, you want them to be evenly distributed. Avoid getting more seams in one area than in another.

You don't want to place multiple seams on top of each other. A few minutes invested in planning your pressing layout will return big dividends. If one seam is pressed to the right, should you press the adjacent one to the right, or to the left? What's going to happen when all the seams come together into a single point? An example of this is the center of a star pattern miniature. How can I press the seams to distribute them equally? These are questions that you should think about. Since each miniature is different there are no hard and fast rules. However, a good rule of thumb to apply is that the wrong side of the finished block should be symmetrical. The pressing layout should look pleasing, with seams complementing each other. There should be no bulkiness in any localized areas. If there is, you will undoubtedly see it when you quilt your miniature.

In star-pattern miniatures that have a central piecing point, the pressed seam allowances will usually flow in the same direction. Looking at the wrong side, the seam pressing will be clockwise or counterclockwise. You will notice in the pattern section, I have included the pressing sequence for each project.

Matching Center Points

You must have matching center points in your miniature or full size quilt. Fortunately, there is no magic involved in doing this. Much of your ability to match center points rests with the precision of your cutting and sewing. I cannot overemphasize accuracy in these phases. It is almost impossible to "work in" dissimilar size pieces so all the points will match.

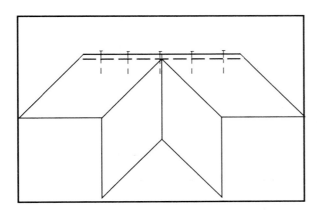

Assuming all of your pieces are cut properly, the following techniques will assure you of good results. Be sure your seams are all pressed in the same direction. Now, lay half of the star on top of the other half, with the right sides facing each other. Take care to butt the seams together so they are tight against each other. The slight offsets in the individual seams should fit together. Be sure the points match perfectly. Now, pin exactly as shown here.

Leave the pins in during sewing. This method gives perfect results if you take care. Rarely do I have to rip out!

Ripping Out

To paraphrase Shakespeare: To rip or not to rip, that is the question. Everyone dislikes this word, including me. No matter how careful you are, mistakes will happen. What should you do? I tell students that it's a personal decision. For me, I know that I will not be happy with my project. Whatever time it takes to redo something is small. I think of the permanence that comes with completion of the quilting.

Some words of caution when you do rip out a seam. Don't use a seam ripper. Seam rippers will stretch and distort your little pieces. I use a small pair of very sharp, pointed surgical scissors. The procedure is to clip the thread every inch on the top side. Then turn the piece over to the back side. You should be able to gently pull the bobbin thread out. Use the tip of the scissors (not the cutting point) to get it started. Your fingernails will do the rest. This method keeps from stretching your pieces. Once you get used to doing it this way, you will find out how fast and efficient it is.

The A-B-C's of Quilting a Miniature

Readers of *Miniature to Masterpiece* will be familiar with the quilting techniques that have served generations of quilters very well. Fortunately, only slight adaptation is necessary for miniature quilts. First, I'd like to elaborate on your choice of batting.

I laugh every time someone asks me about my first quilt. Besides telling them about its array of fabrics, I'll tell them about my batting. I didn't use any; at least nothing that is called batting! Grandma Garrison, my early mentor, always used a flannel sheet between her quilt top and backing. So that's what I used. Later, in 1984 when I became serious about quilting, I met Jeanne Wilber at the Strawberry Patch Calico Shop. Jeanne opened a whole new world to me; and has since become one of my most valued friends. I never realized there are so many types of batting. It's downright confusing. Anyone asking for a roll of batting will get a rude awakening. After extensive experiments, I found that Mountain Mist 100% polyester batting works really well in miniature quilts. It gives my miniatures a bit of a flat look, which isn't "puffy". This is very desirable. An even flatter image may be had by pulling off the top layer of this batting. I use this extensively on certain miniatures when I want to reduce the three dimensional look. Another good friend, Debbie Grow, came up with the batting separation technique. She has quilted hundreds of miniatures for me.

Now let's swing to your choice of quilting needles for miniature quilting. I use a size 10. After getting used to this size, you will think that you're using a crowbar if you go to a larger needle. The size 10 will pierce the fabric weave without having to push its way through. I always use a size 10 for hand sewing, as with applique. Remember the smaller the needle, the smaller the stitch. We are making miniatures!!

Another aspect is the choice of stab or running stitches, or machine quilting. You may use any technique on miniature quilts, of course.

Traditionalists will go for the hand stitching. If you can do the stab stitch, you will be able to quilt even in the heaviest of seams. This maintains a constant stitching pattern. Running stitch quilters will usually have to skip catching the back where you butt the seams together. Functionally, this is of little importance.

Many students have shown me miniatures that they have machine quilted; and they looked wonderful! This is a nice alternative if you are pressed for time, or don't enjoy hand quilting. My guidance here is to keep your stitching as straight as possible, and avoid heavy sewing machine tension. Harriet Hargrave's excellent book on *Heirloom Machine Quilting* is a good reference if you will be doing machine quilting.

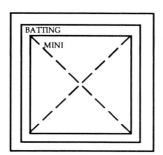

If you do not already own one, you will need a hoop to hold your miniature during quilting. I have always done all of my quilting in a 14" or 16" lap hoop. Miniatures are no exception. In fact, this is the easiest way to quilt them. Prepare to quilt your miniature in this way. Put the miniature top, batting and backing together in a sandwich. Next, run a few large basting threads through the three layers.

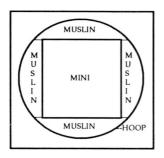

For the third step you will pin four 6" wide strips of muslin around the whole miniature - one per side. Each strip should overlap the miniature's backing by about 1/2" to 1". This means that about 5" to 5 1/2" of muslin will extend outward from each of the sides of the miniature. It is this fabric that you will catch in the hoop. When you put your miniature in the hoop you will see that its entire surface is in view. You can, and should, align all of your blocks as you quilt so everything looks straight. Where do you start quilting? Usually in the center, working outward and straightening your seams as you go.

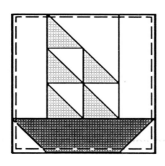

Naturally, the choice of quilting pattern is up to you. Don't over do it! Generally, I only quilt "in the ditch" around the blocks. Some of you may not be familiar with this terminology. It means that the quilting will be next to the seam lines, opposite the side that has the pressed seam allowance. If you do a lot of quilting inside the block, you will distort the pieces.

Miniature Quilt Binding

When I think of bindings I remember a beautiful painting I once saw. It was a scene of early Americana; the artist's depiction of an event from one of James Fenimore Cooper's famous historical novels. The figures in the painting had good proportion, the scale was right and the colors were well coordinated. Its effect caused me to recall many of the details of the scene in the novel. But it was the frame that made the painting really memorable. It had a simple, hand carved wooden border that set the artist's work off to perfection.

And so it is with quilt bindings. The binding should add to the visual effect of the miniature. You must coordinate and execute it well. Otherwise, the effect will be opposite. This is unfortunate, but true.

Thoughts on Bindings

Virtually all of my binding is done in dark color shades. The only exception would be a binding for a miniature that has been done in light shades. Here, a dark binding may have too much contrast. Hence, I might choose a medium or even a light shade for the binding.

I often repeat the use of a piecing fabric, in the binding. Its effect is to tie everything together. Certainly, this is not mandatory. Its just something to keep in mind as you select your binding fabric.

After you have finished with the quilting, trim any excess batting and backing so all three layers are even. This is where I use the 15" square Omnigrid Ruler. Use your rotary cutter to trim.

How To Bind

I cut my binding for miniatures in strips, 1 1/8" wide and 44" long. I make sure the strip is cut crossgrain, or perpendicular to the length of fabric in the bolt. After cutting my strip, I will press under 1/4" as uniformly as I can. After pressing you will have a strip that is 7/8" wide by 44" long.

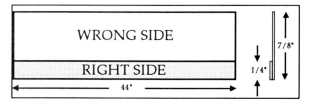

Now, if you have made a non-directional miniature, you will have to decide on its top and bottom. This orientation is important because the bottom is where you will place the seam in your binding. Don't leave it to chance. Hold the miniature up and look at it. How does it look? Decide how you will display it to best advantage. Once again, the bottom is where you want the binding seam.

Next you will pin the unpressed edge of the binding to the miniature. Start in the center of the bottom and work toward your right or left. Be sure to pin in one inch spacings; and stop pinning about 1/4" from the corner. Your pins should be perpendicular to the length of your binding strip. This is shown in the following diagram.

What size seam allowance should you use to attach the binding? It will vary depending on the thickness of your miniature - type of batting, etc. You will have to determine this for yourself. 3/16" is usually a good seam allowance.

Now you will sew your binding to the miniature. Start sewing about one inch from the end of your binding, and stop 1/4" from the corner. Be sure to back tack; trim your threads neatly. See Figure 6.

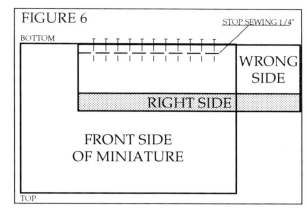

FIGURE 6

STOP SEWING 1/4"

BOTTOM

WRONG SIDE

RIGHT SIDE

FRONT SIDE OF MINIATURE

TOP

The next step is to make two folds, which are easily understood once you see them. Refer to the following diagrams:

Fold your binding up and away from the miniature as in figure 7. Next, fold your binding down. You want to keep all four layers (binding, miniature top, batting, backing) even on the bottom and side edges. Refer to figure 8 to see this step.

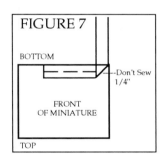

FIGURE 7

BOTTOM

--Don't Sew 1/4"

FRONT OF MINIATURE

TOP

Once again, you will use pins to attach the binding to the side edge of the miniature. Be sure to pin in one inch spacings, with your last pin 1/4" from the top corner. Be sure the unpressed edge of your binding is even with the edge of the miniature. Next, sew as before, starting where you left off (1/4" from the corner). You should stop sewing 1/4" from the corner, and back tack.

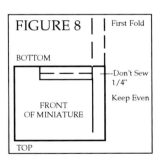

FIGURE 8

First Fold

BOTTOM

--Don't Sew 1/4"

Keep Even

FRONT OF MINIATURE

TOP

Do the corner folds exactly as shown in figure 7 and figure 8. You will continue to attach the binding, using this method, until you come to your starting point. At the starting point on the bottom, overlap the binding slightly and cut off any excess. Whipstitch the binding ends together.

To finish your binding, all that remains is to fold it over the edges of your miniature. Slip stitching will be done by hand, taking care to insure that ripples do not form. Also, your needle should not go through the backing into the top of your miniature.

If you follow this procedure, your binding will complement your miniature to perfection. The 45 degree corner miters will be accurate, adding a touch of professionalism to your project. Now your miniature is complete!

Miniature Full Size Quilts

In this section I will share my latest work with full size miniature quilts. Recently, in two widely separated locations, folks asked me why anyone would make quilts that contain thousands of pieces. My answer? Why not?!!! Women and men have always challenged themselves to work faster, better or in greater numbers. Since quilting first came on the scene, people have yearned for increasingly complicated patterns. Contemporary quilts are one tangent to satisfy this desire. Miniature making is another; here the complexity comes from the accuracy and precision required of the maker. And, if one miniature block is a challenge, how about many blocks pieced together? It was this new challenge that led me to make these full size miniature quilts.

In 1988, my husband and two sons travelled to the Black Hills of Wyoming. They were gone for two weeks and I had extra time on my hands. I had already developed a pattern for a Bear's Paw miniature. Also, I had been thinking about the Bear's Paw within a Bear's Paw for some time. Everything fell into place, and I went ahead. The quilt "Wyoming©" on page 36 was the result.

It took about three weeks to make the main body, and another few weeks to design the border. There are over 6000 pieces in this quilt, and a total of 440 miniature Bear's Paws. Was it a challenge? Yes. Was it fun? Definitely!! "Wyoming" showed me that miniatures can be objects in themselves, as well as a springboard into new aspects of the quilting art. Being a leader in this movement has been especially gratifying to me.

"Never Again", my next quilt, is featured on the cover. You will also find it on page 45. I based "Never Again's" pattern on 45 degree angles. They proved to be a bit tricky to work with, hence the name of the quilt. I must confess that I coined the name early on. About half way through the top, I developed a good method of piecing which really made it easier. However, I stayed with the original name. "Never Again" is a variation of the traditional Lone Star pattern. This quilt contains over 2500 three quarter inch diamonds. It was a great study of color. It has won three ribbons in national competition.

My fourth quilt, "The Exchange©" was named to remember two exchange students who shared our home during the summer of 1989. Alex and Frederic showed a lot of interest in my quilt teaching career. We spent long hours talking while I designed and sewed on this quilt top. I love the many variations of the kaleidoscope pattern. This is my idea of what one looks like in miniature form. There are over 8000 pieces. Each block measures 2 3/4" square. There are 20 pieces in each star block, and 12 pieces in the connecting blocks. All together, there are 761 blocks in this quilt. "The Exchange©" includes over 200 different shades of blue. Many girls throughout the United States sent me these blues. Perhaps the quilt's name has a secondary origin. In effect, it's a sincere thank you to these many friends who were generous with me. Jokingly, I refer to many of my miniatures and quilts as S.O.S. quilts. S.O.S. means Save Our Scraps!

As I write this, I have several other full size miniature quilts on my flannel board and in my head. The flannel board ones have more substance. I've already cut their pieces and placed on a flannel sheet that covers one wall of my studio. The mental ones haven't progressed that far yet; the ones on the flannel board have to move off first!! And move they will. Despite working on this book, I continue to make time to work on my miniatures and quilts.

To conclude this section and the book, I would like to review why I have taken time to write *Miniature to Masterpiece.*

I've received many requests for my secrets to miniature making, so it was time to share my special techniques with you. As I said before, I know the discouragement and frustration that comes from trying to put patterns together that just won't. This book will prevent problems, so they don't arise. Therefore you will not be spending time trying to figure them out. Everything in *Miniature to Masterpiece* will work for you.

Finally, my biggest reason for writing this book is and always will be to share my love of quilting. I hope you have found this love woven into these pages.

Nancy

WYOMING© 74" x 87"

LONE STAR
13 1/4" x 13 1/4"

LONE STAR
15 1/2" x 15 1/2"
Made by Romayne Bonk,
(a student)
Big Flats, New York

COUNTRY SCHOOL HOUSE 9" x 9"
9-PATCH *on the diagonal* 9" x 9"
PINE TREE 8" x 8"

SUMMER SAILING
7 3/4" x 10 3/4" (left)
PINE TREE
8" x 8" (right)
4-PATCH SAMPLER
7 1/2" x 7 1/2" (front)

The EXCHANGE©
This quilt contains over 8000 pieces.
There are 761 blocks to complete the
quilt. It was half quilted when this
photo was taken.

The EXCHANGE© (top)
SCRAPPY GEESE
10 1/4" x 10 1/4" (bottom left)
PINWHEELS WITHIN A SQUARE
(bottom right)

VICTORIAN WALLPAPER© 1989
10" x 10"
The album block squares are 3/8"
square.

KALEIDOSCOPE
12 1/2" x 12 1/2"
There are no curved pieces
in this pattern!

BEAR'S PAW
9" x 9"
*A traditional block sewn
in Amish colors or
Country colors.*

PIONEER CHURN DASH
7" x 9 1/4"
*Two totally different ways of
setting your churn dashes
together.*

GRANDMA'S HOUSE ON A HILL
10" x 10 3/4"

3-PATCH SAMPLER
7 1/2" x 9" (left)
9-PATCH
9 1/2" x 9 1/2" (middle)
This miniature contains 137 pieces
and 41 colors were used. The nine
patch pieces are 3/8" square
BASKETS
10 1/4" x 10 1/4" (right)

A collection of pinwheels
PINWHEELS ON THE DIAGONAL
(left)
PINWHEELS IN MOTION
8" x 9" (middle)
PINWHEELS WITHIN A SQUARE
(right)

OHIO STAR
9 3/4" x 9 3/4"

THOUSAND PYRAMIDS
9 3/4" X 10 1/4" (left)
There are 86 different colors in this miniature.
BIRDS AND TREES
8" X 9 1/2" (right)

SIX PATCH CHARMER
13 1/4" x 18 3/4"
A delightful blend of six different blocks.

NEVER AGAIN 75" x 75"

~Pattern Section~

Six Patch Charmer

Photo Page 44
Overall Size: 13 3/4" x 18 3/4"
Block Size: 4" square finished
Seam Allowance: 1/4"

Supplies:
- Various scraps in light, medium and dark shades for all the blocks and cornerstones
- 1 quilter's quarter (18" x 22") for lattice strips
- 1 quilter's quarter for border
- 1/2 yd. for backing and binding

CROSSES AND LOSSES

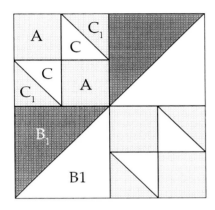

A - Cut 4 - 1 1/2" squares of medium.

B - Cut 1 - 2 7/8" square of light. Cut in half diagonally.

B_1 - Cut 1 - 2 7/8" square of dark. Cut in half diagonally.

C - Cut 2 - 1 7/8" square of light. Cut in half diagonally.

C_1 - Cut 2 - 1 7/8" square of medium. Cut in half diagonally.

1. Sew C to C1. Press seam toward the medium color. Make 4 sets.

2. Sew B to B1. Press seam toward the dark. Make 2 sets.

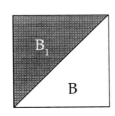

3. Sew A to the C unit. Add the B unit.

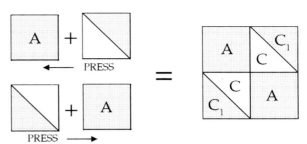

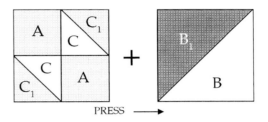

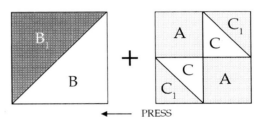

4. Sew the two rows together

WINDMILL

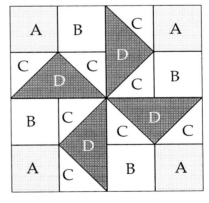

A - Cut 4 - 1 1/2" squares of medium.

B - Cut 4 - 1 1/2" squares of light.

C - Cut 4 - 1 7/8" squares of light. Cut in half diagonally.

D - Cut 2 - 2 1/4" squares of dark. Cut in half diagonally.

1. Sew A to B. Press toward the light. Make 4 sets.

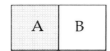

2. Sew C to each side of D. Press to the light.

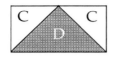

3. Sew the A-B unit to the C-D unit. Make 4 sets. Press up to the A-B unit.

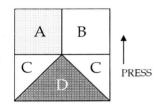

4. Assemble according to the diagram.

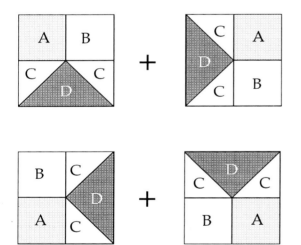

5. Sew your two rows together.

VARIABLE STAR

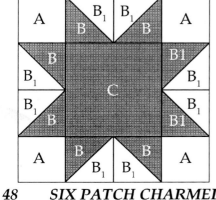

A - Cut 4 - 1 1/2" squares of light.

B - Cut 4 1 7/8" squares of dark. Cut in half diagonally.

B_1 - Cut 4 - 1 7/8" squares of light. Cut in half diagonally.

C - Cut 1 - 2 1/2" square, dark.

1. Sew B to B1. Make 8 sets. Press 4 to the light and 4 to the dark. (When sewing the rows together, use one B set pressed to the light and one B set pressed to the dark. That way you can butt the seams together.)

2. Arrange according to the diagram.

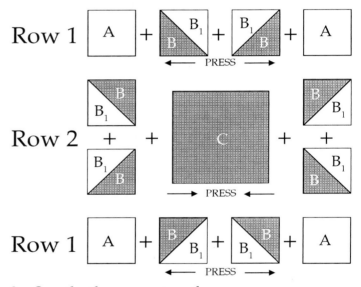

3. Sew the three rows together.

WHIRLIGIG

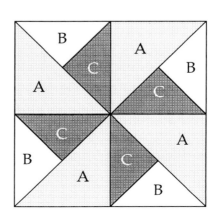

A - Cut 2 - 2 7/8" squares of medium. Cut in half diagonally.

B - Cut 2 - 2 1/4" squares of light. Cut in half diagonally.

C - Cut 2 - 2 1/4" squares of dark. Cut in half diagonally.

1. Sew B to C. Make 4 sets. Press to the dark.

2. Sew A to B-C unit. Press to A. Make 4 sets.

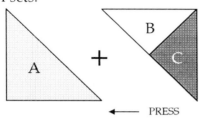

← PRESS

3. Arrange units according to the diagram.

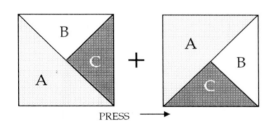

PRESS →

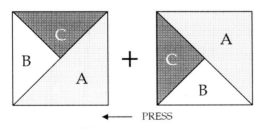

← PRESS

FLYING GEESE

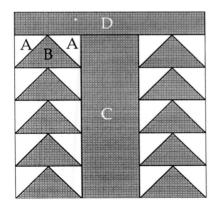

A - Cut 10 - 1 5/8" squares of light. Cut in half diagonally.

B - Cut 5 - 1 7/8" squares of dark. Cut in half diagonally.

C - Cut 1 - 1 3/4" x 4" strip of dark.

D - Cut 1 - 1" x 4 1/2" strip dark.

1. Sew one A to each side of B. Press seams away from the goose (B).

Make 10 geese. After sewing and pressing, if necessary trim the top of the geese to within 1/4".

2. Sew 5 geese together to make a row. Make 2 rows. Press in direction of arrow.

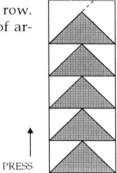

PRESS

3. Sew the C piece between the 2 rows of geese. Press to C piece.

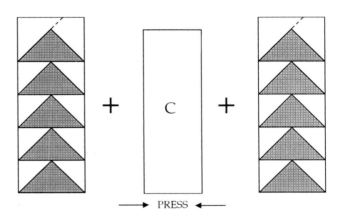

→ PRESS ←

4. Sew D piece to top of the geese unit. Press to D.

SAILBOAT

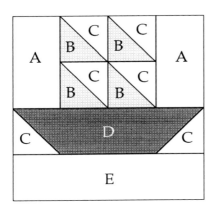

A - Cut 2 - 1 1/2" x 2 1/2" strips light.

B - Cut 2 - 1 7/8" squares medium. Cut in half diagonally.

C - Cut 3 - 1 7/8" squares light. Cut in half diagonally.

D - Cut 1 - 1 1/2" x 5 1/4" strip dark.

E - Cut 1 - 1 1/2" x 4 1/2" strip.

1. Sew B to C. Make 4. Press to B.

2. To make the sail unit:

Row 1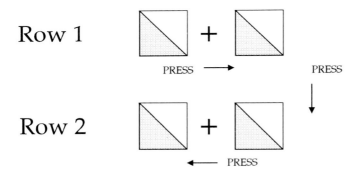

Sew row 1 to row 2. Press seam down.

3. Sew one A to each side of the sail unit.

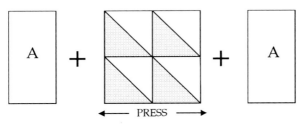

4. Bottom of Boat.

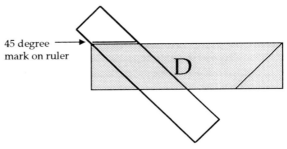

Put the 45 degree angle mark of the ruler on the top of D piece. Make the 45 degree cut.

5. Sew one light C to each side of the boat. Press seams away from boat bottom.

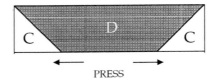

6. Sew sail unit to bottom of boat. Press seams toward boat bottom.

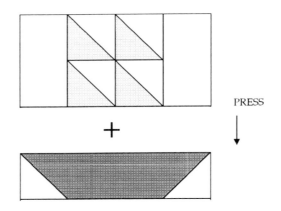

7. Sew E to the bottom of boat. Press seam to E.

___

Measure the blocks. Mine measured 4 1/2" square.

Lattice Strips - Cut 7 - 1 1/2" x your measurement.

Cornerstones - Cut 2 - 1 1/2" squares.

Assemble according to the diagram. Press all seams toward lattice strips.

Row 1:

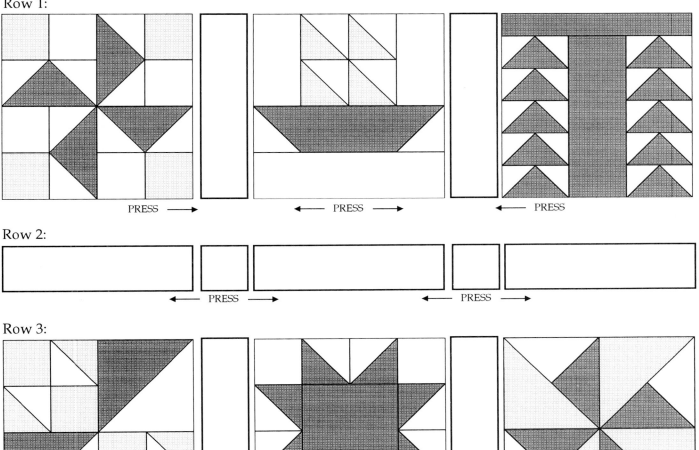

PRESS →   ← PRESS →   ← PRESS

Row 2:

← PRESS →   ← PRESS →

Row 3:

PRESS →   ← PRESS →   ← PRESS

Sew row 1 to row 2; add row 3.

Border I
•Cut 2 - 1 1/2" x size of the miniature. Sew to sides. Press seams to border.

•Cut 2 - 1 1/2" x size of the miniature. Sew to top and bottom. Press seams to border.

Border II
•Cut 2 - 2" x size of the miniature. Sew to sides. Press seam to border.

•Cut 2 - 2" x size of the miniature. Sew to top and bottom. Press seam to border.

Ohio Star Miniature

Photo Page 43
Overall Size: 9 3/4" x 9 3/4"
Block Size: 3 1/8" square finished
Seam Allowance: 1/4"

Supplies:
- ·1/8 yd. light for background, lattice strip and binding
- ·1/8 yd. for the stars
- ·1/8 yd. dark for lattice strips
- ·1 - 12" square for backing

The Ohio Star Procedure

1. (A) Cut 1 - 1 5/8" x 44" strip, light
   (A₁) Cut 1 - 1 5/8" x 44" strip, dark

Position the light strip on the top of the dark strip, right sides together. Cut the strips into 1 5/8" squares. You will need 16 squares of each color.

Recut the squares in half diagonally to make triangles.

2. Sew the light and dark triangles together. Take care not to sew them together wrong.

Press seams to the dark fabric.

3. Join the pieced units together as shown to form a square. You need 16 of these pieced squares.

It doesn't matter which way you press this seam.

4. (B) Cut 16 - 1 9/16" x 1 9/16" of light background for corners. (9/16" is between 1/2" & 5/8")

5. (C) Cut 4 - 1 9/16" x 1 9/16" squares of dark for centers.

6. Sew and press according to the following diagram.

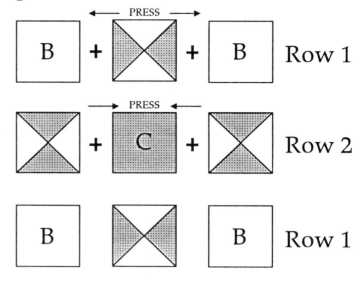

Press seams out to "B" piece on Row 1.
Press seams in to "C" piece on Row 2.

7. Sew row 1 to row 2. Press seams away from row 2. Add another row 1 to row 2. Press seams away from row 2.

8. Lattice strips and cornerstones:
   Cut 1 - 7/8" x 44" strip, light
   Cut 2 - 7/8" x 44" strip, dark
   Cut 9 - 1 5/8" x 1 5/8", dark for cornerstone

9. Sew one dark strip to the light strip. Press seam to the dark side - being careful not to stretch the strip.

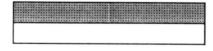

Sew one dark strip to the light strip. Press to the dark side. DO NOT STRETCH THE STRIP!

10. Measure your Ohio Star. It should be 3 5/8" x 3 5/8". If it is not, then you will need to cut your lattice strips to match the size of your blocks.

11. From the pieced lattice strip cut 12 pieces 3 5/8" long (or whatever your star block).

12. Assemble according to the following diagram:

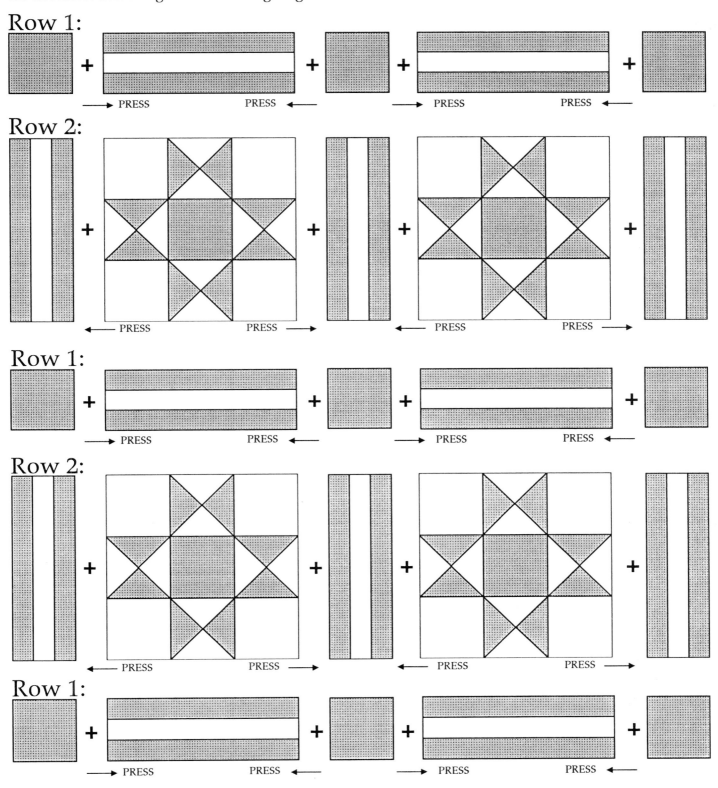

13. Sew row 1 to row 2; add another row 1; add another row 2; ending with another row 1. Press all seams to the lattice strips (row 1).

Pinwheels In Motion

Photo Page 43
Overall Size: 8" x 9"
Block Size: 1 1/4" square finished
Seam Allowance: 1/4"

Supplies:
·Scraps in three different colors for the pinwheels
·Various scraps for lattice strips and first side border
·Small scrap for top and bottom border
·1 Quilter's Quarter (18" x 22") for second side border, backing and binding
·Small scrap of light for background

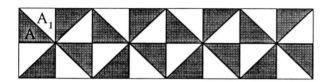

To Make 4 Pinwheels of One Color

1. Cut 1 - 1 1/2" x 14" strip, light
    Cut 1 - 1 1/2" x 14" strip, dark

Position the light strip on top of the dark strip, right sides together. Cut the strips into eight 1 1/2" squares.

Recut the squares in half diagonally to make triangles.

2. Sew A to A1 on the diagonal. Press seams to the dark.

3. Assemble pinwheels according to the diagram. Press seams to dark.

Row 1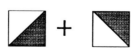

Row 2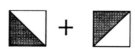

4. Sew Row 1 to Row 2. It doesn't matter which direction you press the center seam.

5. Sew the four pinwheels together, turning every other pinwheel around so you can butt the center seams together.

(The center seam will face up on two of the pinwheels and down on the other two)

6. Make two more rows of pinwheels for a total of three rows.

7. Measure your strip of pinwheels.
    Mine was 5 3/4" long.

8. Lattice strips
    ·Cut 8 (different colors) 1" x your measurement

Sew 2 lattice strips together

Make four sets

9. Assemble according to the diagram. Press all seams toward the lattice strips.

10. Borders
Side Border I:
·Cut 2 - 1" x your measurement. Sew to each side. Press seam out.

Side Border II:
·Cut 2 - 1 1/4" x your measurement. Sew to side. Press seam out.

Top and Bottom Border:
·Cut 2 - 1 1/4" x your measurement. Sew to top and bottom. Press seam out.

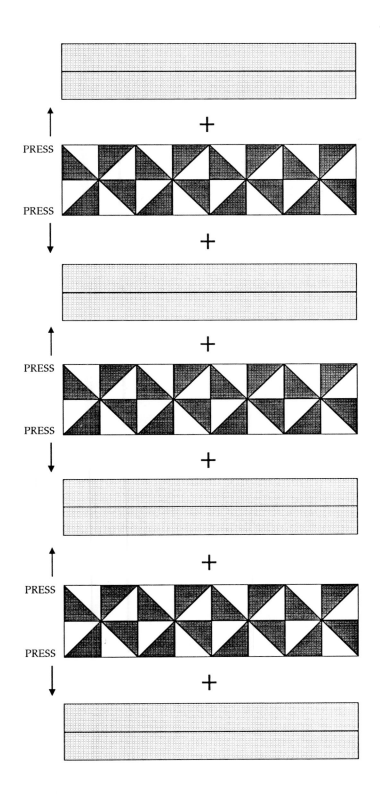

Pioneer Churn Dash

Photo Page 41
Overall Size: 7" x 9 1/4"
Block Size: 1 1/2" square finished
Seam Allowance: 1/4"

Supplies:
- ·Various scraps for Churn Dashes
- ·1 Quilter's Quarter (18" x 22") for background and first border
- ·1 Quilter's Quarter for solid squares and triangles
- ·1 Quilter's Quarter for last border and backing
- ·1 strip 1 1/8" x 44" for binding

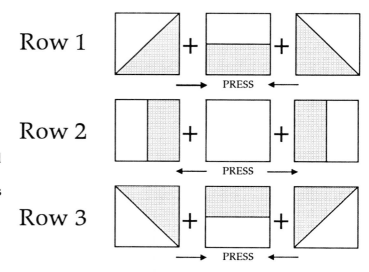

Row 1

Row 2

Row 3

PRESS

To Make <u>ONE</u> Churn Dash

1. A - Cut 2 - 1 3/8" squares, dark
    A₁ - Cut 2 - 1 3/8" squares, light
Cut the squares in half diagonally to make triangles.

2. Sew A to A1 on the diagonal. Press seams to the dark. Make four of these.

3. B - Cut 1 - 3/4" x 6" strip, dark
    B₁ - Cut 1 - 3/4" x 6" strip, light
Sew B strip to B₁ strip. Carefully press seams open. Recut into four 1" pieces.

4. C - Cut 1 - 1" square, light

5. Assemble according to diagram.

DIAGRAM NOTES:
·Row 1 - Press seams to B section. The two seams will just meet in the middle.
·Row 2 - Press seams to B section, overlapping the one dark seam.
·Row 3 - Press seams to B section.

6. Sew the rows together. Press seams to the center. The two seams will just meet in the center.

By pressing all the seams the way I have shown, you will create a nice stable block.

7. Make 5 more blocks in various colors.

8. Measure your block. Mine measured 2" square.

9. Solid Squares
Cut 12 squares the size of your Churn Dash block.

10. Assemble in rows according to the diagram. Press all seams away from the Churn Dash block.

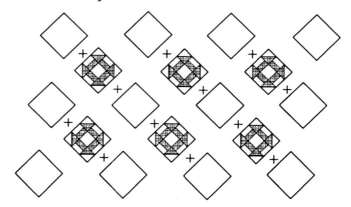

11. Sew the rows together.

12. To "Square-up" - Position your 15" Omnigrid® square ruler on the top and the one side of the miniature.

Make sure the 1/4" yellow line on the ruler lines up on the points of the Churn Dash block.

Cut off the excess and you will have a perfect 1/4" seam allowance all around the miniature.

13. Borders
Border I:
·Cut 2 - 1" x size of the miniature. Sew to each side.

Press seam out.
·Cut 2 - 1" x size of the miniature. Sew to top and bottom. Press seam out.

Border II:
·Cut 2 - 1 1/4" x size of the miniature. Sew to sides. Press seam out.
·Cut 2 - 1 1/4" x size of the miniature. Sew to top and bottom. Press seam out.

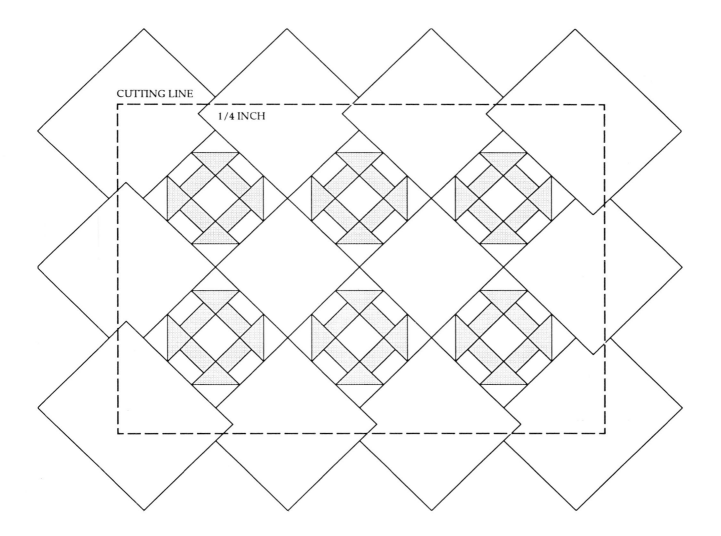

Birds and Trees

Photo Page 44
Overall Size: 8" x 9 1/2"
Block Size Tree: 2" square finished
Block Size Geese: 1/2" x 7/8" finished
Seam Allowance: 1/4"

Supplies:
- Lots of scraps of homespun and plaids for the tree. Scraps of four different prints for the background. Small scrap for the geese. Small scrap background for around the geese.

- 1 - Quilter's Quarter (18" x 22") for lattice and inner border.

- 1 - Quilter's Quarter for last border, backing and binding.

1. To make the tree:

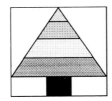

Cut 8 - 1" x 6" strips of different plaids. Sew 4 plaid strips together, alternating dark and light colors.

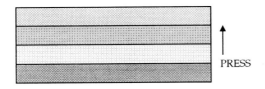

Press after sewing on each row very carefully to avoid stretching. Press all strips in the same direction. Make 2 sets.

2. To make the tree template:

Draw a rectangle 2 1/4" x 3" on heavy cardboard. Mark the center at the top of your rectangle. Draw a line from the center top diagonally to each bottom corner. See diagram.

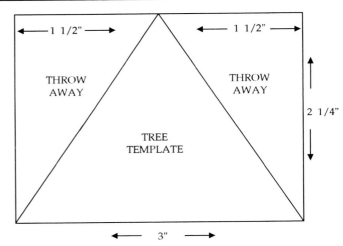

3. Place the tree template on the sewn strips of plaid, keeping the bottom of the template even with the bottom of the strip.

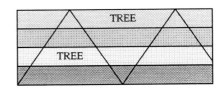

Cut around the cardboard template. Turn the template up side down and cut again. See diagram. Cut 2 tree tops from each set. All four tree tops will now look different.

4. Background around the trees:

B - Use 4 different prints. Cut 2 ea - 1 3/4" x 2 5/8" rectangles. Recut in half diagonally.
You will have more B pieces than you need.

5. Sew one B piece to each side of the tree top. Press seam away from tree top.

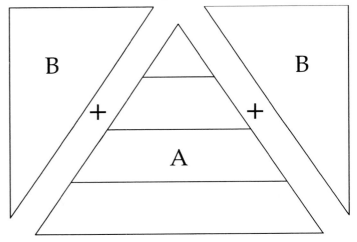

6. Background around trunk:

C - Cut 2 - 1 1/4" x 1" of your four different prints.

7. Trunk:

D - Cut 4 - 1" x 1" of different browns.

8. Sew one C piece to each side of the trunk. Press seams toward the trunk.

9. Sew the tree top section to the trunk section. Press seams to the tree top section.

10. Geese:

E - Cut 1 - 1 1/2" x 12" strip. Cut into 1 1/2" squares.

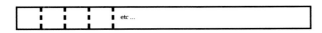

Recut in half diagonally. You need 9 geese.

11. Background around the geese:

F - Cut 9 - 1 3/8" squares. Recut in half diagonally.

12. Sew one F piece to each side of the goose piece (E).

Press away from the goose. Be careful when pressing that you don't stretch the pieces. After sewing and pressing, if necessary, trim the top of the geese to within 1/4".

Your unfinished geese should measure 1" x 1 3/8".

13. Sew your geese together in a row. Press seams in direction of arrow.

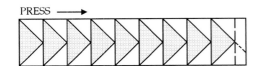

A row of 9 geese sewn together must measure 5" long.

14. Lattice strips:

Cut 2 - 1" x 2 1/2" pieces.
Cut 2 - 1" x 5" pieces.

Follow the diagram for attaching the lattice strips. Press all seams to the lattice strip.

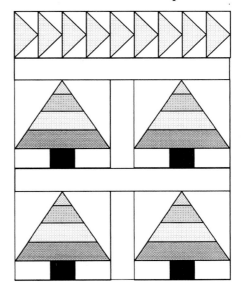

Border I

Cut 2 - 1 1/4" x the size of your miniature. Sew to sides. Press away from tree block.

Cut 2 - 1 1/4" x the size of your miniature. Sew to top and bottom. Press away from tree block.

Border II

Cut 2 - 1 1/2" by the size of your miniature. Sew to sides. Press away from first border.

Cut 2 - 1 1/2" x the size of your miniature. Sew to top and bottom. Press away from first border.

Summer Sailing

Photo Page 38
Overall Size: 7 3/4" x 10 3/4"
Block Size: 2 1/2" square finished
Seam Allowance: 1/4"

Supplies:
- ·1/8 yd. light for background
- ·1/8 yd. medium for sails
- ·Small scrap for boat bottoms
- ·Small scrap for lattice strips
- ·Small scrap for cornerstones
- ·1 Quilter's Quarter (18" x 22") for border,
  backing and binding

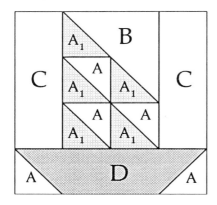

1. To Make The Sails
   A - Cut 1 - 1 1/2" x 24" strip, light
   A₁- Cut 1 - 1 1/2" x 24" strip, medium

Position the light strip on the top of the dark strip, right sides together. Cut the strips into 1 1/2" squares. You will need 15 squares of each color.

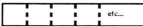

Recut the squares in half diagonally to make triangles.

2. Sew on the diagonal only 18 of the light and medium triangles to make a square. Save the other triangles for later.

Press seams to the medium fabric.

3. Follow the diagram to assemble the three rows of the sails.

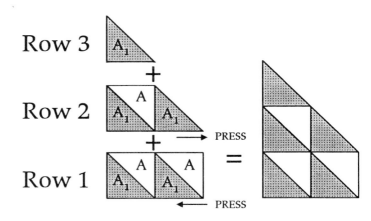

4. (B) - Cut 3 - 2 1/8" light squares. Recut in half diagonally to make 6 triangles. Sew 1 triangle to the sail unit. Press seam to B piece.

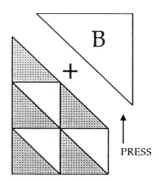

5. (C) - Cut 12 - 1 1/8" x 2 3/8" light rectangles. Sew according to the diagram. Press seam to "C".

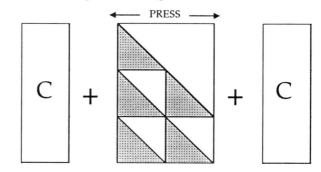

6. Bottom of the boat.
   (D) - Cut 6 - 1 1/8" x 3 3/4" dark rectangles. Put the 45 degree angle mark of your ruler on the top edge of the rectangle. Make the 45 degree cut.

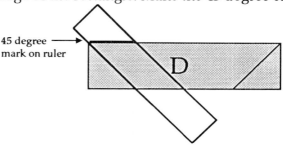

Sew one light (A) triangle to each side of the boat. Press seams away from boat bottom.

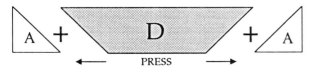

Attach sail unit to the bottom of the boat. Press seam toward the boat bottom.

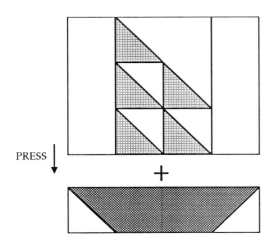

7. Lattice strips.

   Cut 17 - 1" x the size of your block.

8. Cornerstones.

   Cut 12 - 1" squares.

9. Sew lattice strips, cornerstones and blocks together in rows as in diagram. Then sew rows together. Press all seams toward the lattice strips.

10. Borders.

Cut 2 - 1 1/4" x the size of your miniature. Sew to sides. Press out from the sailboats.

Cut 2 - 1 1/4" x the size of your miniature. Sew to top and bottom. Press out from the sailboats.

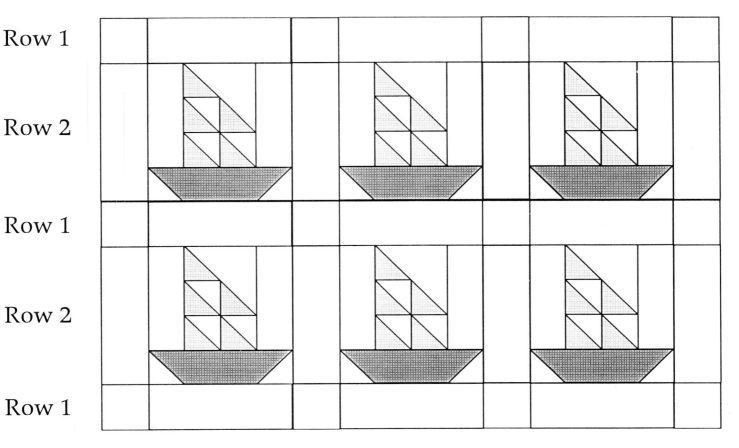

Row 1

Row 2

Row 1

Row 2

Row 1

Country School House

Photo Page 38
Overall Size: 9" x 9"
Block Size: 2 1/2" square finished
Seam Allowance: 1/4"

Supplies:
- Various scraps in light, medium, dark for the house
- 1 quilter's quarter (18" x 22") light for background
- Scrap for lattice strips and first border
- 1 quilter's quarter for last border, backing
- 1 - 1 1/8" x 44" strip for binding

Assemble School House in rows.

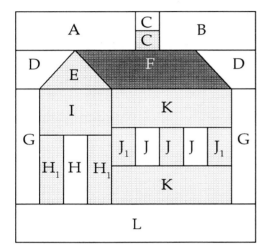

Row 1
Row 2
Row 3
Row 4

ROW 1

A - Cut 4 - 1" x 1 3/4" background
B - Cut 4 - 1" x 1 1/2" background
C - Cut 1 - 3/4" x 5" strip for background
    Cut 1 - 3/4" x 5" strip medium

Sew C strips together. Press to the dark. Trim seam to 1/8". Cut into four 3/4" pieces.

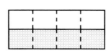

Sew A to C; adding B. Trim seams to 1/8".

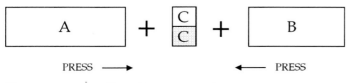

PRESS →   ← PRESS

Press seams to C section.

ROW 2
D - To Make The Template
Cut a rectangle 1" x 1 3/8" from heavy cardboard. Measure in 3/4" on the bottom and put a small dot there. Place your ruler and cut the angle as shown in the diagram.

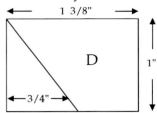

Cut 8 - 1" x 1 3/8" rectangles, light.
Place two rectangles together; wrong sides facing each other. Lay the template on the rectangle and mark the angle line. Cut angle with the ruler and cutter. Separate the two pieces and you will have a D piece for each side of one house. Repeat with the other three sets of rectangles.

E - To Make The Template:
Draw a rectangle 1 1/8" x 1 7/8" on heavy cardboard. Mark the center at the top of your rectangle. Draw a line from the center top diagonally to each bottom corner. See diagram. Using the template cut 4 of medium.

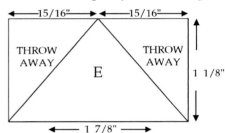

F - To Make The Template:
Cut a rectangle 1" x 2 5/8" from heavy cardboard. Measure in 3/4" on the bottom and 3/4" on the opposite top and put a small dot there. Place your ruler and cut the angle as shown in the diagram. Using the template cut 4, dark.

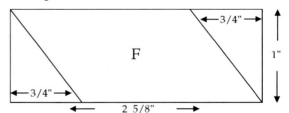

To assemble Row 2:
Sew E to F. Trim seam to 1/8". Press to F.

Sew one D to each side. Press to D.

ROW 3

G - Cut 8 - 3/4" x 1 3/4" background rectangles
H - Door Section - Cut 1 - 7/8" x 6" strip light
H₁ - Cut 2 - 3/4" x 6" strip medium

Sew 1 medium strip to 1 light strip. Press to the medium. Sew other medium strip to other side of light strip. Press to the medium. Trim seam to 1/8". This section must measure 1 1/4".

Cut into four 1 1/4" pieces.

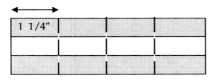

I - Top of door section
Cut 4 - 1" x 1 1/4" medium
Sew to door section. Press to I piece. Trim seam to 1/8".

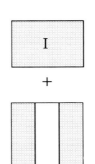

PRESS

J - Window section
Cut 2 - 3/4" x 5", light
Cut 1 - 3/4" x 5", medium
J₁ - Cut 2 - 7/8" x 5", medium

Sew the strips together according to the diagram. Press all seams in the same direction.
Trim seams to 1/8".
Cut into four 1 1/8" pieces.
This section must measure 1 3/4".

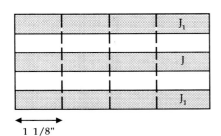

1 1/8"

K - Top and bottom of window section. Cut 8 - 7/8" x 1 3/4" medium. Sew a K piece to the top and bottom of the window section.

Press to the K piece.
Trim seams to 1/8".

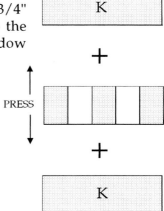

PRESS

To assemble Row 3:
Sew G to door section. Press seam to G piece. Trim seam to 1/8". Add the window section to door section. Press seam to door section. Trim to 1/8".

Add another G to window section. Press to G. Trim seams to 1/8".

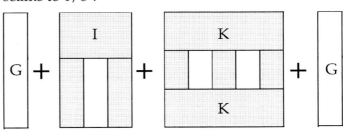

ROW 4
L - Cut 4 - 1" x 3" background.

To assemble complete block:
Sew row 1 to row 2. Press seam up to row 1. Trim seam to 1/8".

Sew row 2 section to row 3. Press seam up to row 2. Trim seam to 1/8".

Sew row 4 to row 3 section. Press seam down to row 4. Trim to 1/8".

The block should measure 3" square unfinished. Otherwise you may have to "square up".

Lattice Strips - Cut 4 - 7/8" x your measurement

Cornerstone - Cut 1 - 7/8" square.

Assemble according to diagram.

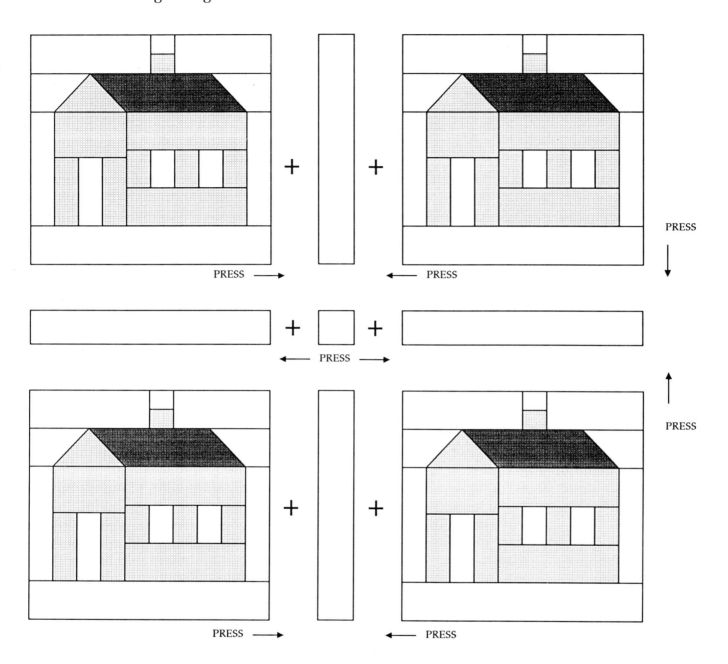

Border I
Cut 2 - 1" x size of the miniature. Sew to sides. Press seams out.

Cut 2 - 1" x size of the miniature. Sew to top and bottom. Press seams out.

Border II
Cut 2 - 1 1/8" x size of the miniature. Sew to sides. Press seams out.

Cut 2 - 1 1/8" x size of the miniature. Sew to top and bottom. Press seams out.

Border III
Cut 2 - 1 1/4" x size of the miniature. Sew to sides. Press seams out.

Cut 2 - 1 1/4" x size of the miniature. Sew to top and bottom. Press seams out.

Lone Star Jewel

Photo Page 37
Overall Size: 13 1/4" x 13 1/4" finished
Actual Star: 8 3/4" x 8 3/4"
Seam Allowance: 1/4"

Supplies:
- ·5 different Quilter's Quarters (18" x 22") for the star and borders
- ·1 Quilter's Quarter light for the background
- ·1 - 15" square for backing
- ·1 - 1 1/8" x 55" strip for binding

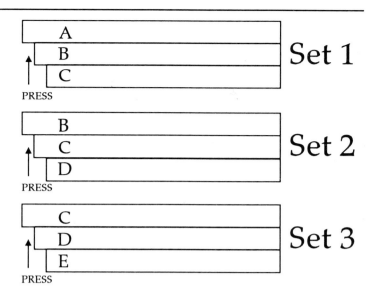

Set 1

PRESS

Set 2

PRESS

Set 3

PRESS

1. Assign a color to each fabric from A through E. This will help keep your colors in order.

2. Cut the following strips cross grain of your fabric.

Fabric A - Cut 1 - 1 1/8" x 17" strip
Fabric B - Cut 2 - 1 1/8" x 17" strip
Fabric C - Cut 3 - 1 1/8" x 17" strip
Fabric D - Cut 2 - 1 1/8" x 17" strip
Fabric E - Cut 1 - 1 1/8" x 17" strip

3. Pin the strips together according to the diagram. The strips are staggered 1" in to allow for maximum use of fabric. Sew set 1 together ... Sew SLOWLY! After EACH strip press in the direction of the arrow. Repeat for sets 2 and 3.

4. Using the 45 degree angle on your ruler as a guide, cut eight - 1 1/8" strips. Repeat for all 3 sets.

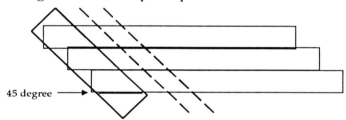

45 degree

When you are cutting your 1 1/8" strips make sure the 45 degree angle runs along the bottom of the strip and the ruler is 1 1/8" in from the cut edge.

NOTE: After cutting two 1 1/8" strips, check to make sure you are still working with a 45 degree angle. You may have to recut a new 45 degree angle on the cut edge.

5. Pin and sew the recut diagonal strips together to form 8 large diamonds. Make sure the diamond points match.

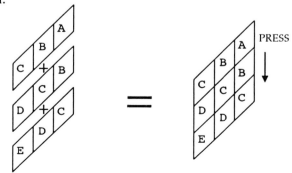

By pressing your seams in the direction shown, you will be able to butt all the seams together when sewing the 8 large diamonds to form your lone star.

6. Sewing the diamonds into pairs.

Take two of the diamonds and pin together, being careful to butt the seams together. Start sewing and stop 1/4" from the bottom edge and back tack. Make four sets.

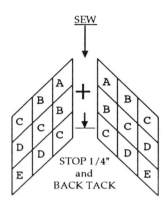

Press the seam to the left. Cut excess tip off.

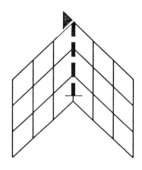

7. Sew two sets together to make a half. Repeat again for other half of star. Press seam to the left.

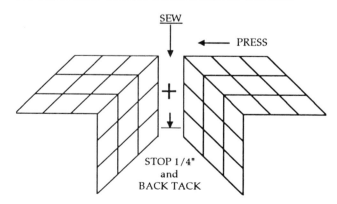

8. Pin the halves together making sure to butt the seams together. Start sewing 1/4" in from the diamond, stop 1/4" from the end of the last diamond and back tack at both ends.

NOTE: Make sure the center seam runs straight across before adding the triangles.

9. Background Squares and Triangles

Cut 4 - 3 1/8" x 3 1/8" squares for corners
Cut 2 - 3 1/2" x 3 1/2" squares. Recut in half diagonally for the triangles.

With the wrong side of the pieced star diamond facing you, pin on the one edge of the background triangle. Start sewing from the outside tip of the diamond. Stop sewing when you reach the 1/4" diamond seam and back tack.

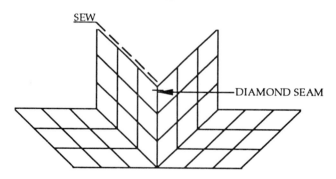

Cut the thread. Remove the star from the machine and pin the background triangle on the other diamond. This time you will be sewing with the background triangle facing you. Stop sewing when you reach the 1/4" mark and back tack.

10. Gently press the seams out from the pieced star toward the background fabric. Cut off the excess tips.

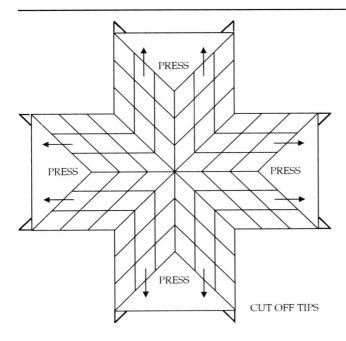

11. Line up the background square with the star. With the wrong side of the star facing you, start sewing. Stop sewing at the 1/4" mark and back tack. Cut the thread and remove from the machine. Pin the other side of the square to the diamond. Now sew with the background fabric facing you. Stop sewing at the 1/4" mark and back tack. Do all four corners this way. Press seams out from the star toward the background fabric.

12. BORDERS
Border I:

•Cut 2 - 1" x size of the star. Pin to the sides of the miniature. Sew with the reverse side of the star up, in order to see where to just miss the star points. Press seams out from the star.
•Cut 2 - 1" x the top and bottom measurement. Pin to the top and bottom of the miniature. Sew with the reverse side of the star up, in order to see where to just miss the star points. Press seams out from the star.

Border II:
•Cut 2 - 1 1/4 x the side measurement. Pin and sew to the sides. Press out from star.
•Cut 2 - 1 1/4 x the top and bottom measurement. Pin and sew to the top and bottom. Press out from star.

Border III:
•Cut 2 - 1 1/2 x the side measurement. Pin and sew to the sides. Press out from star.
•Cut 2 - 1 1/2 x the top and bottom measurement. Pin and sew to the top and bottom. Press out from star.

Scrappy Geese

Photo Page 39
Overall Size: 10 1/4" x 10 1/4"
Block Size: 3 1/2" square finished
Seam Allowance: 1/4"

Supplies:
· Various scraps of light, medium and dark
· 1 Quilter's Quarter (18" x 22") for border, backing and binding
· Small scrap for lattice strips and first border
· Small scrap for cornerstones

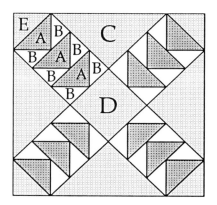

Procedure: To Make <u>ONE</u> Block

A. Geese
   Cut 6 - 1 1/2" squares dark
      Cut in half diagonally.
B. Background
   Cut 12 - 1 1/2" squares light
      Cut in half diagonally.
      (This piece is over sized on purpose.)

1. Sew one B to each side of A. Press away from A. Be careful when pressing that you don't stretch the pieces. Make 12 geese.

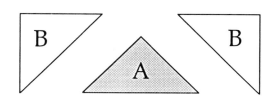

2. After sewing and pressing, trim the top of the block to within 1/4" of the goose. Your geese should measure 15/16" x 1 3/8".

3. Sew three geese together to make a row. Press seam up. Make 4 rows.

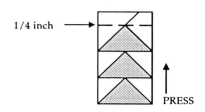

C. Large Triangle
   Cut 2 - 2 3/8" squares. Cut in half diagonally.

D. Large Square for Center
   Cut 1 - 1 3/8" square.

E. Corner Triangles
   Cut 2 - 1 3/4" squares. Cut in half diagonally.

4. Assemble block according to the diagram.

NOTE: Due to minor differences in sewing and cutting, some students use a scant 1/4" seam allowance to assemble this part of the block. You be the judge.

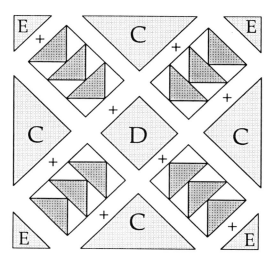

Outside sections, press to C piece. Middle section, press to D piece. Sew corner triangles (E) on last and press out.

5. Make three more blocks in different colors.

6. Measure the square. Mine measured 4" square.

Lattice Strip
   Cut 4 - 1" x your measurement.

Cornerstone
   Cut 1 - 1" x 1".

7. Assemble according to the diagram.
   Press seams to the lattice strips.

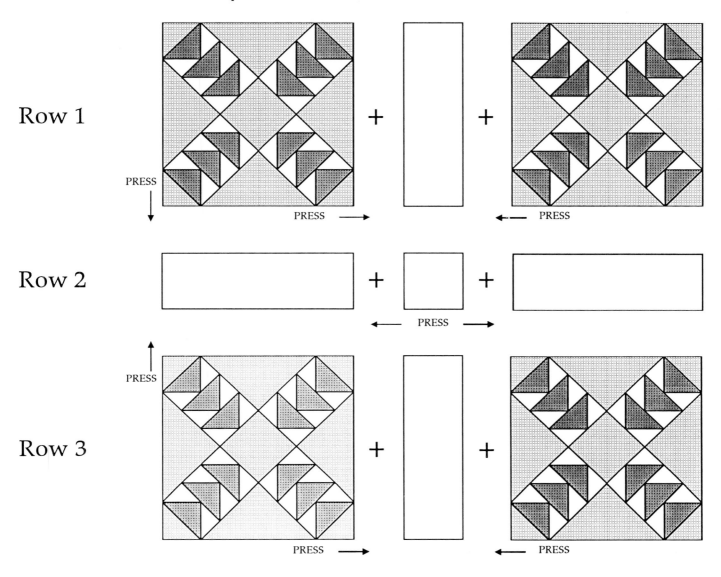

Row 1

PRESS

PRESS ⟶

+

+

⟵ PRESS

Row 2

+

+

⟵ PRESS ⟶

Row 3

PRESS

+

+

PRESS ⟶

⟵ PRESS

8. Borders
Border I:
·Cut 2 - 1" x size of the miniature. Sew to the sides. Press seams out.
·Cut 2 - 1" x size of the miniature. Sew to the top and bottom. Press seams out.

Border II:
·Cut 2 - 1 1/2" x size of the miniature. Sew to the sides. Press seams out.
·Cut 2 - 1 1/2" x size of the miniature. Sew to the top and bottom. Press seams out.

Kaleidoscope

Photo Page 40
Overall Size: 12 1/2" x 12 1/2"
Block Size: 2 5/8" square finished
Seam Allowance: 1/4"

Supplies:
- 1 - 1/4 yd. light for background and first border
- 1 Quilter's Quarter for last border, backing and binding
- Various scraps for the Kaleidoscope points
- Marilyn Doheny 45 degree wedge triangle ruler

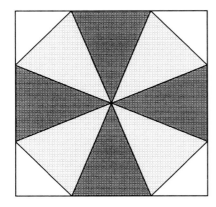

The Kaleidoscope consists of only two pattern pieces. An optical illusion is created by the use of color.

Before beginning, assign a color to each number from 1 through 5 and 5A. Note my suggested colors in parentheses.

When cutting the fabrics with colors 1 through 5, cut a strip 2 1/4" wide by suggested length. Recut using the Marilyn Doheny 45 degree ruler. Turn the ruler upside down every other time.

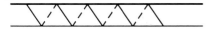

Color Chart:		Strip Size	Recut
Color 1	(green)	2 1/4" x 11"	8 times
Color 2	(burgundy)	2 1/4" x 11"	8 times
Color 3	(blue)	2 1/4" x 25"	20 times
Color 4	(rust)	2 1/4" x 15"	12 times
Color 5	(background)	2 1/4" x 30"	24 times
Color 5A	(background triangle around the Kaleidoscope block)	1 5/8" x 32"	

Recut into 1 5/8" squares. Cut these squares in half diagonally. You need 36 triangles.

When pressing piece 5A, press the four pieces IN on every other block and OUT on the opposite blocks. This will make it easy to butt the blocks together. See #8 for diagram.

To assemble I will use Block A for a sample.

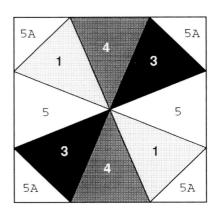

1. Sew color 5 to color 3. Press seam to number 5.

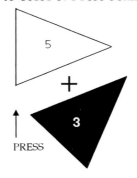

2. Cut off the excess tip.

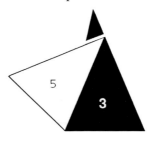

3. Sew color 4 to color 1. Press seam to the left and cut off the excess tip.

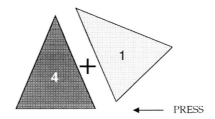

4. Sew the 5-3 section to the 4-1 section. Press seam to the left.

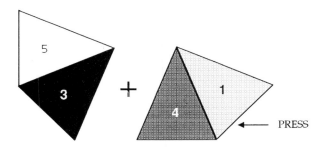

You have made half of the block. Repeat for the other half.

5. Sew the two halves together, matching the center. You will have a diagonal center seam. It doesn't matter which direction you press this seam.

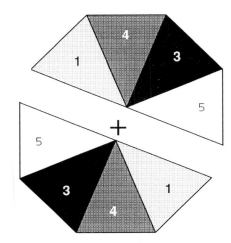

6. Sew the 5A triangles on the proper corners.

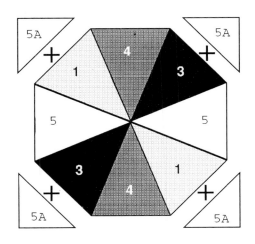

Press the 5A pieces out from the block.

7. Make 9 blocks following the color and pressing chart.

8. Sew into rows according to following diagram.

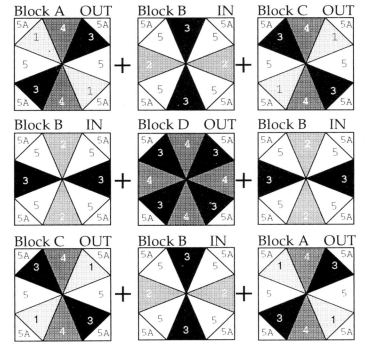

9. Sew rows together.

10. Measure your miniature. Mine measured 8 1/2" square.

11. Borders
Border I:
•Cut 2 - 1 1/4" x your measurement. Sew to sides. Press seams out.
•Cut 2 - 1 1/4" x your measurement. Sew to top and bottom. Press seams out.

Border II:
•Cut 2 - 1 3/4" x your measurement. Sew to sides. Press seams out.
•Cut 2 - 1 3/4" x your measurement. Sew to top and bottom. Press seams out.

Wyoming ©1989 NJS

Photo Page 36
Overall Block Size: 12" x 12" finished
Block Size: 3 1/2" square finished
Seam Allowance: 1/4"

Supplies for one block:
- •1 Quilter's Quarter (18" x 22") light for miniature bear's paws
- •1 Quilter's Quarter dark for big bear's paw
- •1 Quilter's Quarter for background

MINIATURE BEAR'S PAW
Directions are for ONE block.

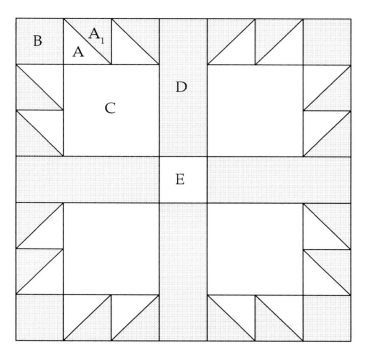

1. A - Cut 1 - 1 3/8" x 12" strip, light
    A1 - Cut 1 - 1 3/8" x 12" strip, dark

Position the light strip on top of the dark strip, right sides together. Cut the strips into 1 3/8" squares. You need 8 squares of each color.

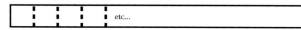

Recut the squares in half diagonally.

Sew A to A1. Press seam to the dark. Make 16 units.

2. B - Cut 4 - 1" x 1" dark
3. C - Cut 4 - 1 1/2" squares light
4. To assemble sew two pieced squares together. Press to the light.

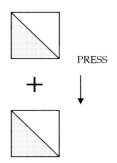

5. Sew this strip to C piece. Press to C.

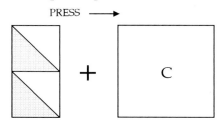

6. Sew two more squares together. Press to the dark.

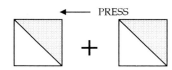

7. Sew this strip to B piece. Press to B piece.

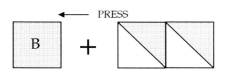

8. Sew to the top of the paw unit. Press to the C piece.

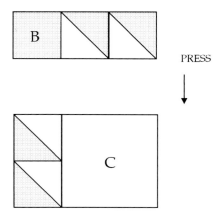

9. Make four identical paws this way.

10. D - Lattice strips - Cut 4 - 1" x 2" dark.

11. E - Cornerstone - Cut 1 - 1" x 1" light.

12. Assemble according to the diagram.

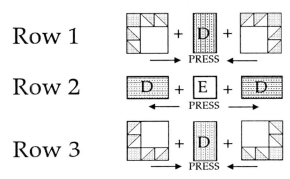

Row 1

Row 2

Row 3

13. Sew rows together to make a complete bear's paw. Press to row 2.

14. Make four complete miniature Bear's paws for each 12" block.

BIG BEAR'S PAW

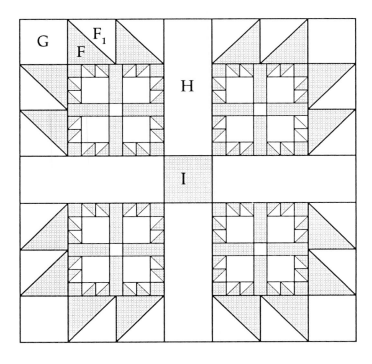

1. F - Cut 8 - 2 5/8" squares, dark. Cut in half diagonally.
   F₁ - Cut 8 - 2 5/8" squares, light. Cut in half diagonally.
   G - Cut 4 - 2 1/4" squares, light.
   H - Lattice strip - Cut 4 - 2 1/4" x 5 3/4" rectangles, light.
   I - Cornerstone - Cut 1 - 2 1/4" square, dark.

2. Sew F to F1 to make a square. Press seam to the dark. Make 16 squares.

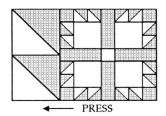

3. Sew two squares together. Press seam down. Then sew to the side of one of the Miniature Bear's Paw. Press seams away from Miniature Bear's Paw.

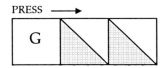

PRESS

4. Sew two squares together. Add G. Press away from G.

PRESS ⟶

G

5. Sew this section to the miniature section butting your seams. Press away from miniature Bear's Paw.

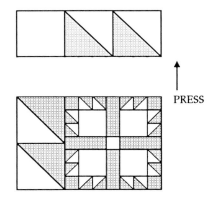

PRESS

6. Make four identical units to complete one 12" block.

7. Assemble according to diagram on next page.

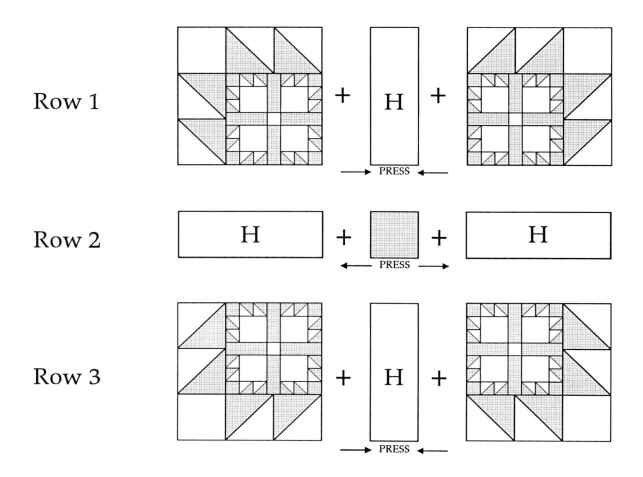

Row 1

Row 2

Row 3

PRESS

8. MINIATURE BEAR'S PAW BORDER
Follow the directions for the Miniature Bear's Paw,
omitting the D and E pieces.

9. From your dark background fabric cut 2 - 1 7/8"
squares. Cut in half diagonally. Sew one triangle to
each side of the pieced block.

Press seams out.

You need 124 of these units.

Never Again
(Miniature Broken Star)

Photo Page 45

Overall Block Size: 20 1/4" x 20 1/4" finished
Diamond Size: 3/4" finished
Seam Allowance: 1/4"

Supplies:
- Fabric A - 1/8 yard
- Fabric B - 1/4 yard
- Fabric C - 3/8 yard
- Fabric D - 1/4 yard
- Fabric E - 1/8 yard
- Background (light) - 1/3 yard
- 4 Large Outside Triangles - 1 quilter's quarter (18" x 22")

This block is made from 32 pieced diamonds.

The following directions will show you how to make <u>one</u> complete broken star using five different colors.

1. Assign a color to each fabric from A through E. (This will help you keep your colors in order.)

2. Cut the following strips cross grain of your fabric.

Fabric A - Cut 2 - 1 1/4" x 44" strips
Fabric B - Cut 4 - 1 1/4" x 44" strips
Fabric C - Cut 6 - 1 1/4" x 44" strips
Fabric D - Cut 4 - 1 1/4" x 44" strips
Fabric E - Cut 2 - 1 1/4" x 44" strips

3. Pin your strips together according to the diagram. The strips are staggered 1" in to allow for maximum use of fabric. Sew set 1 together ... Sew SLOWLY! After EACH strip press in the direction of the arrow.

Repeat for sets 2 and 3.

Set 1

Set 2

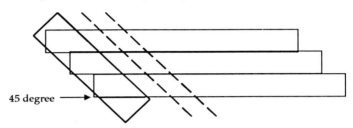

Set 3

4. Using the 45 degree angle on your ruler as a guide, cut eight - 1 1/4" strips. Repeat for all 3 sets.

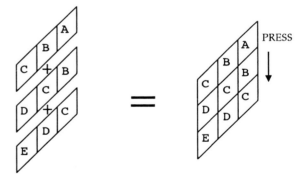

45 degree

When you are cutting the 1 1/4" strips make sure the 45 degree angle runs along the bottom of the strip and the ruler is 1 1/4" in from the cut edge.

NOTE: After cutting two 1 1/4" strips, check to make sure you are still working with a 45 degree angle. You may have to recut a new 45 degree angle on the cut edge.

5. Pin and sew the recut diagonal strips together to form 32 large diamonds. Make sure the diamond points match.

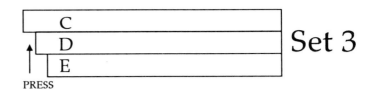

By pressing the seams in the direction shown, you will be able to butt all the seams together when sewing the 32 large diamonds to form the broken star.

6. To make the center star:

Pin together two diamonds, being careful to butt the seams together. Start sewing and stop 1/4" from the bottom edge and back tack. Make four sets.

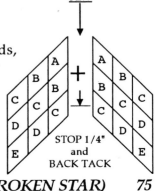

SEW

STOP 1/4"
and
BACK TACK

Press the seam to the left. Cut excess tip off.

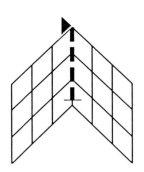

7. Sew two sets together to make a half. Repeat again for other half of star. Press seam to the left.

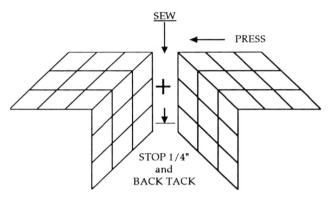

8. Pin the halves together making sure to butt the seams together. Sew 1/4" in from the diamond, stop 1/4" from the end of the last diamond and back tack at both ends.

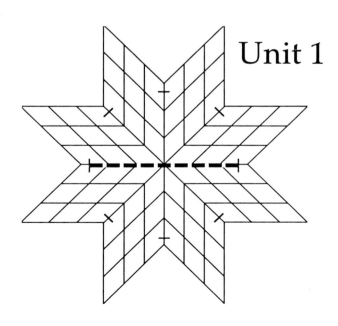

Unit 1

NOTE: Make sure the center seam runs straight across before adding the triangles.

9. F - Background Squares

Cut 8 - 3 1/2" squares, light

10. Following the diagram, sew the diamonds into pairs, being careful to butt the seams together. Stop sewing 1/4" from the diamond edge.

11. To make UNIT 2:

Following the diagram, sew F to the two sewn diamonds first. Press seams to F piece. Attach the center star to F. See diagram. Press seams to F piece.

Attach each Unit 2 this way.

12. To make UNIT 3:

Sew four diamonds according to the diagram. Attach F. Press seams to F piece. Make four Unit 3's.

13. Sew Unit 3 to Unit 2 and the center star as shown. Press seams to F.

14. G - Background Triangles

Cut 8 - 3 7/8" squares. Cut in half diagonally.

Following the diagram, sew G to the star. Press seams to G.

15. H - Large Outside Triangles

Cut 2 - 7 1/8" squares. Cut in half diagonally.

Sew one triangle to each corner. Press to H.

NOTE: The symbol "—" indicates that you should stop sewing 1/4" from edge and back tack.

Problem Solving Guide

PROBLEM	HOW TO PREVENT	HOW TO FIX
A. Fabric Selection		
Cannot distinguish between block pieces and background pieces		
·shade contrast	Plan your shade contrast according to the color choice model	Increase shade contrast between your fabrics (refer to color choice model)
·fabric scale	Watch out for "overpowering" of small scale fabric, especially in adjoining pieces	Change large scale print to medium scale
B. Fabric Preparation		
Fabric is limp after washing	Use Magic® Sizing, or similar product, to restore body	Use Magic® Sizing, or similar product, to restore body
Colors run together after washing your miniature quilt	Always prewash your fabric before using it	Unfortunately, there is no solution to this problem. Prewashing is a must!
C. Layout and Cutting		
Ruler slips when cutting long strips	Use "hand walking" method described in this book - cut in 6" increments	Do not use strips that are not perfect. Cut new strips to replace bad ones
Cut wanders despite using hand walking method	Change cutter blade frequently - it must be sharp	Replace blade and resume cutting
	Use slight pressure against the ruler when cutting	Use slight pressure against the ruler when cutting
	Do not move fabric during cutting. Move the board 180 degrees after making your initial cut to square up	Resquare fabric, rotate board 180 degrees and resume cutting
Strips have a slight, but perceptible, "V" at the fold line	Always resquare your fabric after cutting two or three strips	Do not use strips that are not absolutely straight. Cut new strips and resume your project
Fabric pieces that are cut with a template are too large, or too small	Make sure that your template is exactly on size. Verify your template size by measuring it with your precision ruler. On most templates, you must cut the drawn lines off	Oversize pieces may be trimmed using your ruler and rotary cutter. Do not try to use undersize pieces by adjusting seam width; it's too complicated
D. Sewing and Pressing		
Fabric pieces are mangled during sewing	Use size 11 needle and change frequently	Replace with new size 11 needle

PROBLEM	HOW TO PREVENT	HOW TO FIX
Cannot see needle and stitching during sewing	Replace presser foot with "Applique" foot	Replace presser foot with "Applique" foot
Cannot obtain accurate 1/4" seams	Use the masking tape method described in this book	If using the masking tape method, verify that it is a true 1/4" Make sure you are holding your fabric against the sewing guide on your machine. Insure that your sewing guide has not moved or worn during use
Small fabric pieces fray and become distorted	Use good quality 100% cotton that is tightly woven	
	Do not use steam during pressing. Press gently	Discontinue using steam and/or heavy pressing
Long strips become unsewn after cutting into short strips	Use 10 - 12 stitches per inch	Adjust machine stitch to a tighter pattern (10-12 per inch is recommended)
Chain piecing difficulties	Keep fabric under the needle. Butt squares or rectangles against each other. Overlap triangle tips slightly	Check the position, as indicated. Insure that no gaps exist between the fabric pieces. Stop sewing just before the edge of the piece. Position the next piece and sew to its edge, etc.
Squares made of two triangles distort when pressed	Cut off the tips (dog ears) BEFORE pressing. Press gently	Cut off the tips (dog ears) BEFORE pressing. Press gently
Long sewn seams become crooked when pressed	Always press your sewn seam closed first, then press to the light or dark fabric as called for in the instructions	Repress the seam as indicated
Machine has difficulty sewing over the "hump" created when using pins to hold the pieces	Use a long thin pin such as the W.H. Collins #104 pin	Use a long thin pin such as the W.H. Collins #104 pin
Fabric stretches when ripping out	Do not use a seam ripper! Use small surgical scissors to clip the threads	Discontinue ripping until the surgical scissors are purchased. Distorted fabric will be oversize and will cause difficulties
Perceptible "bulk" in the finished block	Seam allowances must be pressed evenly and symetrically. Multiple seam allowances should not accumulate in a particular area.	Repress seam allowances to distribute evenly

E. Quilting

Quilting stitches are too large	Use size 10 or 12 quilting needle Avoid pulling your miniature too tight in the lap hoop	Quilt a small area and see how it looks. Adjust your quilting stitches accordingly
Quilted blocks look distorted	Plan the quilting to complement your mini. Do not over quilt. When quilting any ultra-small blocks, quilt only "in the ditch"	Quilt a small area to check for distortion. Rip out (with surgical scissors) if necessary, and start over
Miniature looks puffy (too thick)	Use thin batting for any miniature project. See the batting section of this book	Plan ahead! There is no solution to this problem after the quilting is completed

Suppliers

PRODUCT	WHERE TO PURCHASE
Omnigrid® rulers and boards	Quilting stores or: Omnigrid® Inc. 3227-B 164th S.W. Lynnwood, WA 98037
Olfa® rotary cutter	Quilting stores
Sharpie® extra fine point permanent marker	Office or Art supply stores. Some quilting stores
Size 11 sewing machine needle	Quilting stores
Applique Foot	Your sewing machine dealer
1/4" masking tape	Quilting stores
Filament tape	Hardware stores
#104 W. H. Collins fine silk pins	Limited quilting stores
Sharp pointed surgical scissors	Medical supply stores
Mountain Mist® batting	Quilting stores
Size 10 quilting needle	Quilting stores
14" or 16" lap hoop - hand made by Gene Wilber	Mr. Gene Wilber R.D.#3, Box 44 Columbia Cross Roads, PA 16914
All of the items listed above and the bears (by Joyce Reichard - Milton, PA) and dolls (by Judy Grant - Milton, PA)	The Strawberry Patch Calico Shop Jeanne Wilber R.D.#3, Box 44 Columbia Cross Roads, PA 16914 (717) 549-6111

Antiques displayed in photos courtesy of Jeanne Wilber are not for sale.

Baskets displayed in photos by Mary Ann Machey are not for sale.